Tales from Ca

A (mostly) medi

By
Ileana von Hirsch

To my adored family, who don't believe a word I say (and who urge you not to either).

And to Colette Ellis who not only believed me, but inspired me, as well as bringing joy, love and laughter to all around her, right till the end.

"No matter how hard the world pushes against me, within me, there is something stronger, something better, pushing right back." Albert Camus, in a letter to a friend.

Contents

Introduction – Calypso's Embrace

In my previous book, *A Funny Thing Happened on the Way to Chemo*, I described my first adventures in dealing with a diagnosis of stage three breast cancer, its unexpected and rapid metastasis to the liver, followed by life with stage four cancer. Primarily, the point was to share with worried friends and family the surprising treasure trove of laughs I found along the way. With a striking lack of originality, I compared my journey to an Odyssey, which was particularly fitting as I come from the island of Ithaca, the kingdom of Odysseus, from where his Odyssey started, and to where he eventually returned 20 years later. Seven years of this Odyssey were spent – unwillingly we are told – on the magical island of Ogygia, in the seductive embrace of the goddess Calypso.

Unlike Odysseus, I know that I will never return to Ithaca (metaphorically at least, as I do get there quite often at the moment with Ryanair), and my story is rather of life with Calypso in the Ogygia of Cancerland, that strange continent where my ship stranded me.

I still maintain that Cancer is just another country to which one travels, with its languages, customs, food, people, clothes, advantages and disadvantages. As the earlier format of my previous book – beginning, middle and end – is no longer appropriate to my story (apart from an eventual end bit of course), I now see this as a series of reports or postcards from Cancerland, sent back to friends and family as and when something amuses, intrigues or puzzles me. Having done a bit of travel writing in my day-job as a Greek villa agent, this is a format I am very familiar with; observing the quirks of each place visited. The initial wide-eyed amazement and wonderment that propelled me through the first couple of years of exploring a new country has perhaps worn off, but the curiosity and eagerness to understand remains – as does the determination to find as much amusement along the way as possible, and to communicate it to others, so that I enjoy the journey wherever it takes me.

For the past four years I have been someone who is, as they say, "living with cancer". This means that I have a cancer that is incurable, but treatable, so that all things going well, my oncology team can keep me going for a satisfactory number of years. I often compare life in Cancerland to a Harry Potter book; you live in a parallel magic world, whilst still being able to pass for a Muggle and live an ordinary Muggle life. Unlike a Muggle, though, you have an extra dimension and membership of a fascinating club that has access to all sorts of interesting professionals, science, privileges and opportunities. Small but precious benefits pave the road with gold: becoming an author, wheelchairs and minders in airports, seats on trains vacated for you with alacrity, permission to cancel any plans or commitments without any excuse, *carte blanche* to cut to the chase (time is precious), and all sorts of other goodies.

"Do you get a disability card for parking?" asked someone once when I was giving a little talk about this.

"No," I said, "but you could try sticking your Macmillan Cancer Emergency Toilet Card under the windscreen wiper." One just has to be creative with one's situation.

Perhaps the most significant discovery, though, is that of my own power to protect my psychic well-being, so that I live most of the time in an idiot's bubble of happiness and positivity. It reminds me of a camp song that my Canadian mother used to sing to us when we were little:

"Oh, happy little moron, playing in the sand.
I wish I were a moron, Oops, perhaps I am."

We said moron in those days.

Narratotherapy

"You've always had the power my dear, you just had to learn it for yourself."
Glinda the Good Witch in *The Wizard of Oz* (Frank Baum)

My three grown-up children are very strict with me, each in their different way. My youngest son, the Eco-warrior, supervises the

5

environmental credentials of my housekeeping and lifestyle and gives me praise and improving suggestions as and when necessary. The older son, the Lawyer, never shies away from telling me when I am being boring or irritating, or both, and at regular intervals allows me rationed and controlled glimpses into his life; and my eldest, the Emotional Support Daughter, watches Netflix with me, makes sure that I manage the family in the correct way and don't sneak down at midnight to raid the cookie cupboard. What they do all agree on, though, is that I am a terrible attention-seeker, that this is very annoying and is the least attractive side to me. "What you don't realise Mummy, is that when you tell your stories and laugh and dominate conversations, people stop listening. Surely you must understand by now that quiet people get listened to more than loud people."

Not by me they don't, that is for sure. Quiet people irritate me terribly, as I hate having to cup my hand behind my ear and say "What? What did you say? Do speak up," in a dowagery way, while wondering why people can't enunciate properly, and then finding out that what they said was not that interesting anyway and I needn't have bothered.

In any event, as a diminutive, half-Greek, half-Jewish, Alpha female, being a quiet person goes directly against the grain. It is restful silence or entertaining drama, not much in between, so it came as a wonderful release, a liberation even, to find that the "noise" I make not only amuses me, but some other people too.

Friends and other cancer-related people actually ask for my advice and about how I manage to stay so positive, and then say, "You are so brave and inspirational, you are amazing." In fact, I know perfectly well that I am neither brave nor amazing, though it is nice to hear that I am inspirational. I brush such comments off with impatience. I am just, in defiance of my children, doing what I love; entertaining myself and other people, making myself and them laugh, and this, when one thinks about it, is the key to finding happiness in unpromising territory. Reality is a very plastic affair that can be moulded to suit you and allow you to cope with things. In short, the glass half full or half empty is a choice that we can all make, and we can also choose to a certain extent what we put in the glass. We have the power to control the narrative. This is also the key to being able to manage the fears and concerns of friends and family – I insist on going to all doctors' appointments alone, so that, should there be any bad news, I can try out a number of alternative narratives in private; discarding the ones that don't quite work before settling on one that is true but upbeat. This not only allays others' fears and stops them panicking – and, *much worse,* infecting you with their panic – but it also becomes the official narrative for yourself, a sustainable platform upon which you can build. When you get to be a pro like me, it only takes about 15 minutes to get the right narrative, but rather like making pancakes, you need to flip a few before you get a good result.

I discovered, to my pleasure, that somewhere down the line, I seem to have acquired a psychic housekeeper – an in-built Pollyanna who always looks on the bright side and finds things to be glad about, even in the least promising circumstances. My Pollyanna is responsible for keeping all my glasses not only half full, but also sparkling clean. She keeps my brain neat and tidy, busily putting things away, hanging things up, dusting, airing, polishing, washing and ironing, decluttering, recycling the rubbish, defrosting the fridge, arranging flowers and making sure that all is gleaming. A pearl who is the envy of all my friends. Every day she is there when I wake up, and sees exactly what needs to be done, what – if any – mess the night has created that needs dealing with. She is never without her can of Pledge and a duster. There is a carpet in the entrance of my psychic house, under which all morbid thoughts and fears are swept, just because that is the right place to keep them. This is not to hide them or pretend they aren't there, on the contrary, it is precisely so that I know that they are there, but that they are firmly underfoot and under control. I can lift up my carpet any time and inspect what is under there, which one obviously ought to do now and then. It is akin to the skulls painted in the bottom right-hand corners of Dutch Old Masters, a *memento mori* that creates a serene familiarity with death, from which we have, as a culture, become estranged. Whether you are religious or not, we are stardust and to stardust we return. At a short talk I once gave on the subject of psychic under-carpet storage, someone asked me if things didn't simply fester there. This is an important question, and the official answer is yes, of course things fester if left under

7

carpets. A whole counselling, therapy and self-help industry has been built on this. My answer however is no, they don't, as long as you know they are there. Of course, if the carpet starts heaving and moving and you hear squeaks and pattering underneath, see the odd flash of tail, catch a whiff of ammonia or a pool of liquid seeps out, then perhaps you ought to take some drastic measures, but as my brother-in-law said to me at my wedding 31 years ago, speaking about my bridegroom, if it ain't broke, don't fix it.

My daughter, who is much braver than me, and is constantly examining under a microscope every single disturbing or uncomfortable thought until it displaces all else from her mind, did not agree.

"Mummy," she said, "A better analogy for you would be a cabinet. You don't really sweep things under a carpet where you never look at them again, I think you actually arrange things nicely in a cabinet and shut the doors. Now and then you open the doors and check that things are prettily displayed and add new objects that you have collected, having decided where they would fit best, but I think you look at things more often than you would do if they were under a carpet."

Carpet or cabinet, it doesn't make much difference – the main thing is to let your inner Pollyanna get on with her housekeeping and in that way control your narrative.

I call it therapeutic narration, or Narratotherapy, and every time I am faced with Cancer Counselling, which is offered to people living with cancer all the time, I head off the well-meaning, "And how do you feel about having cancer? Do you feel overwhelmed, alone, scared of dying?" conversations with an enthusiastic account of my discovery.

The transformative power of storytelling is something that fascinates me. I had a friend, Sara, diagnosed around the same time as I was, but with a very poor prognosis, to whom I used to send pages as I wrote them, as she said they made her laugh out loud and helped her through the night. I did this right up to the week she died. I mined every day for things to make Sara laugh out loud, and I am still happy at the thought that my rummagings were of comfort to her. The habit of looking for things to laugh at every day has stayed with me, and like any muscle, the brain gets better and better with practice, till it becomes like brushing your teeth – you don't even think about it. My oncologist assures me that laughter is a huge boost to survival rates, and that if he can get someone to laugh at the first appointment, he feels that things will go well.

On the other end of the spectrum are people who refuse to narrate either to themselves or to others. Their psychic houses are in a tragic state of neglect and disrepair. Dirty windows are sealed shut by layers of old paint, rooms are un-aired, dust gathers, rubbish collects, flowers wilt, dirty dishes pile up in the sink, bills go unpaid and finally the power gets shut down. Enough to depress anyone. I had lunch a while ago with a friend who told me about her grandfather – a meek and gentle soul who designed postage stamps and would never have said boo to a goose. After his death, they went over his papers and discovered that he had been married twice before and had various children from his earlier marriages. The fall-out was as incendiary and damaging to all, as one might have expected.

By way of contrast, my father, a larger-than-life Greek with a highly eccentric and flamboyant character, also had had three wives and umpteen children – known and unknown – the difference was that from the time we could sit at a table and hold a knife and fork, he regaled us with stories about his past, and we all listened with mouths wide open in admiration, and eyes bright with amusement as his stories were all hugely funny. We grew up thinking that his adventures and shenanigans were all totally normal. As an adult, I once tried to take a closer look at some of his stories, at least to determine a timeline that made sense. I couldn't, things didn't add up, and I came to the conclusion that there may well have been some smoke and embroidery in order to enhance a good story. What we had in effect was a huge, glittering heap of loose stones – some mega-carat diamonds, some rhinestones – all sparkly, but nothing resembling a strung necklace. Those stories gave everyone enormous amounts of pleasure, even though running like a vein through them were pain, heartbreak, anger, infidelity and exile, which are, when you come to think of it, not very funny at all. Despite this, a mealtime without one of our father's stories was no fun at all and we all begged for one every day. Storytelling is the necessary complement to sweeping things under carpets, rather like those

9

thick black plastic sheets that gardeners lay down in allotments to kill off weeds, while leaving small holes for what they have planted to grow through and up into the sunlight – in other words, story-holes; to control what grows and what dies.

I used to think of my father as the chamois in the old Baby Cham television advertisements from the 60s and 70s. Baby Cham was a foul drink, a sort of post-war austerity mock champagne. In the advert, a grey and dull scene was brought to technicolour life as a cartoon baby chamois bounded joyously across the screen, leaving in his wake a sparkling trail of rainbow colours and bubbles. That was the effect my father had on the world. I remember once, long after his death, visiting a place we used to clamour to visit with him as children, a duty-free alpine resort just over the border from stuffy Switzerland where we holidayed, into chaotic and vibrant Italy. It was the highlight of the year and a day trip there was the apogee of glamour, fun, excitement and beauty. We used to smuggle miniature bottles of *Goldwasser* and *Kirsch* back into Switzerland in our ski-gloved fingers, squirming with suppressed giggles as we passed under the noses of the Swiss border guards. We didn't really understand the concept of duty-free at that age...

I went there on my own some time after his death, and to my astonishment, the place was an absolute dump (though still duty-free). Now, I am not saying that Cancerland is a dump, God forbid, but it is true that stories, and the storytelling urge, can transform anything. Rainbows, sparkles and bubbles whenever you want.

I do realise that I am in a very privileged position; my children are grown up, I have a supportive family, lovely friends, no pressing financial worries, an understanding boss, (I run my own company) and am the holder of a very thorough German health insurance policy who pony up like lambs and send me a Christmas card every year – so it is really not too hard for me to see the funny side of things. I don't even feel particularly unwell most of the time. I wouldn't presume to set myself up as an example or role model to others in different circumstances. We all do our best and whatever helps us is good, and whatever makes us feel bad is to be avoided. I simply wish to share my experience of how one can control one's narrative, which helps me though everything that has so far been thrown at me.

The Art of Superficiality

My daughter lives life on a far more metaphysical and spiritual level than I do (she tells me that this is because she is a Capricorn with Scorpio ascendant and Moon in Uranus and Pluto). She has always been profoundly intuitive, in tune to the invisible and philosophical world, and despairs at my stunted spiritual growth and lack of curiosity. As one gets older, she says, it is a shame not to also become more profound, to look into life more deeply. Sadly, I have no intention of deepening anything at all – on the contrary – I am developing a Philosophy of the Surface. I aim to rehabilitate superficiality, to make 'skin-deep' a term of praise. After all, skin is the only interface between us and the world. If the surface is well-maintained and lubricated, wear and tear is reduced and the "deep" machine can work smoothly. At the most basic level, an individual cell only exists due to a protective membrane, separating it from the biological soup around it, giving it an identity as a cell and enclosing and protecting the contents within. Without that skin, there is no cell, and therefore no plant, animal, water, no star or sun, only undifferentiated *stuff*. So why is superficiality so looked-down-upon? Take care of the surfaces, and what goes on underneath can largely be managed.

A Very Acceptable Quality of Life

On the subject of managing things, "a very acceptable quality of life" is what Prof E, my oncologist, aims to give me, as he said when explaining that metastasised cancer is technically incurable – but not to panic. I think that a very acceptable quality of life is a rather good result for anyone, so all in all, a very acceptable state of affairs. In fact, when he asks me, as he does every time I see him, "How is your quality of life?" I say, "very acceptable," and he smiles happily.

Your daily routine consists of managing your energy, refusing in the nicest possible way to allow negative or unrewarding things into your life, building in plenty of exercise, learning to delegate, living healthily and consuming vast amounts of kale and broccoli (good) to offset the 4.30 pm chocolate biscuits (bad). In fact, I run a sort of carbon-offsetting scheme, nutritionally speaking of course. How much kale do you have to eat to offset:

a)   A bad quality chocolate biscuit
b)   A good quality 100 % cacao square of chocolate
c)   A sticky toffee pudding
d)   A cinnamon Danish?

The kale-diet methane emissions rates must also be factored in. My son, who works at a large consulting firm in the sustainability and renewable energy department, once worked on a similar accounting project for a small Central American country.

On Being an Author

Taking up residence in Cancerland had an unexpected result, one that made me extraordinarily happy, namely, the beginning of a new job – that of being an author. I wrote *A Funny Thing Happened on the Way to Chemo* during the first year after I was diagnosed. I was lucky enough to find Short Books as publishers, who are blissfully eccentric and chilled. They edited lightly but firmly, patiently cutting out all the tasteless bits, and pretending not to notice when I snuck them back in again.

While not wishing to knock my day-job in any way, (which involves painstakingly hand-selling expensive Greek villa holidays to demanding clients), for attention-seeking extroverts like myself, having a book published is a totally joyous thing, and makes the promised quality of life much more than just acceptable – it makes it an absolute blast.

Before going to print, I gave Prof E the draft of my book to approve. He is going to be the most important man in my life for ever now, so the last thing one wants is to write something he would not like. Luckily he was beyond enthusiastic, saying to his secretaries as I was standing there, "You must read this, it is a real hoot! I took it to bed with me to read and fell asleep." I tried unsuccessfully to get this printed on the back cover as one of those blurb reviews. No, said Short Books, with unusual firmness.

There is a slight hitch, though, now that he has read it. In my last appointment, he was explaining something to me, then suddenly stopped and looked at me warily, "Are you still writing? Because I am now not sure if everything I say won't end up in a book."

"No, no," I promised him insincerely, "Everything you say is completely confidential."

The *Daily Mail* agreed to publish an excerpt before the book came out, as anything to do with women and boobs gets disproportionate attention in the *Mail,* so I tick all the boxes. Goodness knows how men ever get anything published. "We will send a photographer," they wrote, "please make sure you don't wear black or jeans, and we need the Jack Russell on your lap and your husband in the picture as well."

I told them I could probably round up the Jack Russell unless she was on one of her tours around the Borough of Harrow, but I wasn't sure what old-school Bavarian gents like my husband would think about appearing in the *Daily Mail*, assuming he had ever heard of it.

The old-school Bavarian gent was, as it turned out, thrilled to be photographed for the *Daily Mail*, which he had never read of course. He dressed very carefully that morning, putting on his too-short yellow trousers and a salmon pink shirt.

"You can't wear those!" I protested, "The colours clash and the trousers don't fit."

"But this is how I always dress," he replied, truthfully.

The photographer, when he turned up, clearly thought he had been sent to do a "Lost dog returns to family" scoop.

13

"Where's this famous dog then?" he asked. I had to explain that it was all about me, bravely surviving a horrific disease, not about a dog.

He looked a bit disappointed, but a job is a job, so he unpacked his camera, took one look at my husband's outfit, and said, "Just the dog, I think."

"I told you so," I said to Florian, who never listens to my comments on his dress sense.

***

Once you are published, nice things start to happen. First of all, there is the box of complimentary books that arrives from your publisher. You immediately fill a whole shelf with your Oeuvre and admire the spines with your name on it for days. You can hardly bear to give any away as the display looks so nice. "Buy your own copy," you snap at kind friends who ask for one, "I only have 30 in stock, which I need to keep the shelf looking nice, so you had better order from Amazon – and please leave a good review when you do." I have figured out how to say this kindly though, with a pious – and truthful – "Good reviews are important as it makes the book more visible online, and therefore easier to find for any people who might need cheering up."

On a hot Friday afternoon, brimful with happy anticipation, I stopped off at the surgery of my GP, Dr H, to give him a precious signed copy of the book.

"I have a little present for Dr H." I said proudly to the receptionist.

"I see," she said in a surprisingly ungracious way, "He won't be in till Monday now, so I suppose I will have to keep it here," and then gave me a dirty look. I pulled out the book and handed it over to her. "Will you give this to him on Monday then please?"

"Oh, a real present!" she exclaimed, "I thought it was going to be a urine sample, and they don't keep very well over the weekend in this heat..."

My children finally plucked up the courage to read my book and see what was written about them. My daughter Danae wants to go on record as saying that I have largely invented the

14

catalogue of things she has collected/treasured/rescued from rubbish bins over the years, that she is not in the slightest bit odd or weird, and that most people would love to have a daughter who is as concerned about their mother as she is about me. She is quite right. She has also been teaching the Greek members of the office English phrases and idioms like "to be hard done by", and "slander". I had to explain to them that English culture frowns upon praising one's children in public. They looked at me in Greek incomprehension, and my daughter smiled smugly.

"It is a sign of love," I explained to them, "I wouldn't want to make people jealous by showing them how brilliant, charming, clever, hard-working, affectionate, beautiful and cultured my children are, and how much I love them."

"Ah, British irony!" one of the Greeks exclaimed, pleased to have finally spotted it after I have been trying to explain it for years.

"No, no, I am being sincere," I said, "I really do think my children are wonderful and love them more than anything else." He shrugged his shoulders as if to say, "If you say so…"

The Lawyer son, following my entirely loving and admiring portrait of him in my previous book, has asked me to clarify that he is not really on the autistic spectrum, and made only one comment:

"My girlfriend was not long-suffering. If anything, I was." She is, at the time of writing, his ex-girlfriend. The Eco-warrior son, after asking me to stop calling him the Eco-warrior, just gives me special hugs now and then, after telling me off for throwing away glass bottles instead of putting them out to recycle and says that he appreciates that I am making more of an effort. They did all unite to add, "For someone who is in marketing and supposed to be such a whizz at selling, you are not doing a great job on your children. All three of us single. And your book will not help. In fact, it will reduce to zero your chances of grandchildren. It is a Catch-22 – any decent romantic prospect will read your book out of interest and a desire to please us, and then drop us like a hot potato after they read your character assassinations."

My children really are all beautiful, intelligent, sensitive, educated, funny, healthy, affectionate, self-supporting, conventional and morally upright. Any takers, please write to Short Books...

***

I made it my mission to get Daunt Books on Marylebone High St, "The most beautiful Bookshop in London" to stock my book. They specialise in travel books, and as I pointed out, my book is largely all about travelling – Cancerland, Harley St – whichever way you look at it. They said "Oh how interesting" very politely and continued not to stock it. As I passed by there every three weeks, they really didn't stand a chance. To begin with, I would go in and ask anonymously if the book was in stock, and when they said no, I would say sniffily that I would order it from Amazon. Then I started going in and ordering it, (giving a false name in case they noticed that the name on my credit card was the same as the author's name, which would have been a bit embarrassing). Eventually they started to recognise me, so I had to stop doing that. One day though, my efforts paid off. I went in, under my own name and asked if they had a copy, and after a search ("Hmm... how strange, someone seems to have put it under "Humour"") there it was, on a stand, next to John le Carré and Penelope Lively, and just when I thought life could not get any better, the store manager said to me "We have three copies, would you be kind enough to sign them? We do like our authors to drop by and sign their books". I do feel that my literary career cannot get better than that. I have achieved the maximum.

Literary Life

A philanthropic group of Greek ladies living in London very generously offered to host a fund-raising for the wonderful Maggie's Centres, whose buildings have been designed for free by world class architects, and which offer cosy and supportive drop-in centres for anyone touched by cancer. They invited me to read some passages from my book, after which I signed copies to give to the donors. The turn-out was mostly Greek, many with

16

some connection with breast cancer – either friends had it, or family, or they themselves.

I chose the funniest bits I could, and while there was some laughter, there was a surprising amount of people wiping tears from their eyes. Afterwards, as I sat there signing books, I was horrified at the number of people who came up to me holding out their copy, gulping and saying, "Oh, that was so moving, you are so brave".

"No, no," I replied, "It is not moving, it is just funny! Laxatives are moving, this is not, I want to make you laugh, not cry!"

"No," they all insisted, "it is moving." So I gave up and tried to look brave and inspiring. Hard for me as I am not a very empathetic person, nor am I easily moved, except for some very odd moments that I don't understand myself. I was told a story at a funeral in Germany, during which I stayed totally dry-eyed, about someone's grandfather who, as an 18-year-old on the Russian Front in the winter of 1945, was trying to make his way back to Germany. Cold, frightened and hungry, his most prized possession was a woolly sweater his mother had knitted for him, and which he had managed to hang on to throughout the Russian route. One day he took it to the river to freeze off the lice with which it was infested. Then, suddenly, the call came to move on, and he had to leave his mother's woolly sweater in the frozen Russian river and drag himself on, westwards, with the rest of the weary boys. This made me sob for about ten minutes, and for about a month after, all my family had to do to reduce me to tears was to say mournfully, "Oh, the poor woolly sweater left behind in a frozen Russian river". Whether it is the thought of the mother waiting, not knowing, hoping the sweater was keeping her son warm, or the son, crying for his mother next to a frozen Russian river... oh dear, here I go again....

Florian said to me by way of consolation, that any 18-year-old in 1945 would have been volunteered for service by Hitler-supporting parents, as boys weren't being drafted anymore, so really it serves the mother right.

However, as I said, apart from some peculiar patches of emotional wiring, not much makes me cry, so when people thank me and insist with wet eyes that my book is moving, I just give in and say that I am so glad they like it.

**

There is a flip side, of course, to going public. The editor of a rather highbrow magazine asked if he could print an excerpt from what I was writing (i.e. this book). "Such a fan!" he gushed.

The sub editor was not unfortunately. He found Pollyanna too whimsical. Did I want to do some editing, or would I like to leave it to them? I was outraged. Whimsical? No one has ever called me whimsical in my life, nor anything that I have said or done. I am the most unwhimsical person I know. Then the doubt set in. Perhaps it *was* time to get rid of Pollyanna. I had to remind myself that the point of writing was to take away stress and create good cheer, not to get angry. I have a day-job for that.

I replied nicely that I would leave it to them.

The Literary Festival

I was kindly asked to do a reading at a little gem of a literary festival called Stuckeridge.

A week before the date was due, my friend John, who runs events and speaker evenings, told me with unusual (for him) severity, "You can't possibly just sit there and read, it is hugely discourteous, and I don't allow it at any of my events. It is a pity, because as a first timer, you will find it very difficult to speak for an hour." Panic set in. I am incapable of learning anything by heart, let alone learning something by heart *and then reciting it in public*. Three years ago, in an attempt to ward of Alzheimer's (no longer a concern luckily as I am sure that the Big C will get me first), I bought a brilliant book called *A Poem a Day* – 365 short poems – which I placed by the loo and resolved to learn by heart, poem by poem, one a day. I still haven't been able to memorise even the first line of the poem for day one, a poem I love, and I go to the loo at least eight times a day. My husband has got used to hearing from behind the bathroom door, "Of all the vices, no, virtues, no, *vices*, that conspire to blind / man's erring, erring, man's erring something, man's erring, oh *bollocks!*" Not quite what Alexander Pope had in mind. A little learning is indeed a dangerous thing.

I spent a week in anguish trying to learn my six densely written pages of notes, on the verge of playing the cancer card and cancelling. In the end I threw away my notes and just told a lot of jokes, and the friendly audience was so relieved that it wasn't a gloomy talk about chemotherapy, that they laughed at absolutely everything I said, even the serious bits.

"How do you manage?" I asked some of the other speakers who had mastered the, to me, incredible feat of speaking without notes for 45 minutes with no umms or errs. Lots of practice and beta-blockers seemed to be the general consensus.

The Tuesday Lunch Club

While life as an author has its novelties, some things don't change. The Tuesday Lunch Club, as the cosy lunches at the chemo-clinic with my friends came to be known, with the entirely suitable acronym of TLC, continues to meet, though now every third Thursday rather than Tuesday, (administrative blip on the calendar,) possibly because the clinic has upgraded its menu. I am actually becoming a fixture on friends' "good deed circuits". Laura goes from my chemo cubicle to her voluntary post at Childline, Rosie comes to me from her occasional help with prison play performances, Kate goes on to chair her committees on gambling abuse, and Mark goes on to his Zen meditation and charity trustee meetings. "Visiting sick friend" for a quick cup of tea and a healthy salad of burnt broccoli and cashews fits in nicely.

The most popular date by far was the pre-Christmas Day session, when exhausted friends staggered up the stairs to the third floor, collapsed into a visitor's chair, hinted that they too might like their blood pressure measured and some drugs dripped into them, and moaned about the Christmas shopping crowds. You, of course, have been shopping solidly all year on

Marylebone High St every third Thursday, as a little treat post chemo, so have finally joined the elite group of smug people that you used not to be able to stand, who say irritating things like "I finished my Christmas shopping in August and the only present I have left to do is my brother-in-law's youngest niece's best friend's dog-walker." My own favourite TLC is the one just after Christmas. It is my spa day – a day of self-indulgence, putting your feet up, telling people about your aches and pains, and having cups of tea and sandwiches brought to you, followed by some gentle physio. And not a jingle bells in earshot.

Of course, the huge advantage that oncology clinics have over spas is that you get really first-class drugs. Lucy, a Lifer like me, and I were sitting side by side having treatment and comparing notes on how we manage to get our drugs of choice – Zopiclone for me and Xanax for Lucy – in whatever quantities we like. "Well, there are my NHS GP and my private GP for starters, then Prof E is always good for a month's supply, and the clinic doctor here as well." The clinic reflexologist working on my feet in a cloud of whale sounds, lavender and tea tree oil nearly fell off her stool in horror. We fixed her with beady eyes, "What goes on in Vegas stays in Vegas" Lucy told her sternly.

The Cardiologist

One side effect of a less pleasant drug that I take, is shortness of breath and heart pounding. In other words, where you used to sprint up the stairs in an underground station, rudely pushing aside slower or baby-/suitcase-/pushchair-encumbered mortals with an impatient hiss of annoyance, you now cling to the railing and haul yourself up the last few steps behind the artificial hip replacements, the diabetics on walking sticks and ten-month pregnant women, then have to stop, gasping, at the top. If you are unlucky, they will exchange sympathetic looks with you. Where you saunter into an Oncology clinic with your head held high, looking around to make sure that everyone can see how your nonchalant air speaks of years of inspirational Battles Against Cancer and how very high status you are in Cancerland, the Cardiology clinic is an entirely different matter. It is full of old people and you can't help feeling that no one speaks of victims of heart disease. They speak of old-age, over-eating, too much wine and too little exercise. You slink in with your collar turned up, hold a newspaper up to your face and hope that you won't be spotted by anyone you know. Cardiology clinics have absolutely no glamour.

It reminds me of the time when I was pregnant with my first child, still un-proposed to by my future husband, no spouse at my side. I was sitting in the obstetrician's waiting room for my first appointment, and to my humiliation, had to sign a form saying that I agreed to have an AIDS test before I would be accepted as a patient. Clearly all un-married mothers were sluts and the doctors were taking no chances. As I was sitting there feeling like an infectious bacterium, a young couple whom I knew walked in hand in hand – pillars of the London-Greek community, and freshly engaged.

"Oh, hello Ileana, we are here to get our blood tests done to make sure we are compatible parents, why are you here?"

"I am having an AIDS test," I said loudly and glared back at them, realising that if Florian didn't marry me, I was lost to the London-Greek market for ever. Luckily, he did.

***

Having said that cardiology clinics are low in medical glamour, there are 20 million women in the UK and USA wandering around with dicky hearts due to their cancer drug regime, and pharma companies are no slouches when it comes to spotting new markets, thank goodness. Cardio-oncologists aren't there to fix your heart, they are there to keep it ticking so you can continue taking your cancer drugs. Their job is to make sure you die of cancer, not heart disease, while your Oncologist is working in direct opposition to make sure that your heart, not cancer is what will finally get you. You could always let them both off the hook by stepping out in front of a bus of course...

Cardio-oncology is bad news for the national health services and insurance companies, who are faced with the double whammy of twice as many expensive consultant bills, tests and medicines, while seeing the presumably hoped-for demise of their clients receding into the distant horizon... Herr Moeginger at Allianz Insurance, *Entschuldigung.* I am so sorry. I did send him a murder mystery book as a thank you, where the serial murderer stalking German hospitals turned out to be a health insurance broker trying to save his firm money by bumping off patients before they had their expensive operations. "Oh," he said in distress when I told him. "I would never dream of doing anything like that, how dreadful!" Germans are wonderful.

Cardio tests done and hooked up to a network of little heart monitors and a bleeper clipped to my waist, I was let loose by Dr L, my brand new cardiologist, for 48 hours so that he could see what was going on. My first stop was the British Museum to see an exhibition of the Parthenon Marbles and Rodin (we don't call them the Elgin Marbles any more). In case you are interested, Parthenon Marbles 1, Rodin 0. I discovered that dangling your heart-bleeper ostentatiously outside your trousers, like a colostomy bag, gets you speedy access to the disabled loos, which is a very good trick as the able-bodied loos in the British Museum are almost as antique and rare as the Parthenon marbles, and the 25-person queue is not in a mood to pay any attention to the "Cancer Toilet Card" that you momentarily consider brandishing. A heart bleeper is a trick well worth adding to any repertoire – and with the help of an old hard drive, a belt clip and a blood-red plastic tube, you can try it too.

At my appointment that afternoon with Prof E, when he asked me how I was, I told him about my cardiologist meeting and showed him my monitor. He gave me a strange look, then slowly began unbuttoning his shirt, looking me straight in the eye. Now, we are good friends, Prof E and I, especially since he knows that I write about anything that he says, but this was unexpected. Of course, he has seen my chest hundreds of times, but I hadn't yet seen his.

"Look!" he said, and sure enough, he had little heart monitors clipped to him as well. "Routine check" he added, after I asked him whether I should be looking for a new oncologist. Compassionate, that is me.

The next day, my first stop was for lunch with an ex-boyfriend, the first big love of my life, who broke my heart as a

20-year-old, and whose voice used to make my heart race almost unbearably and my knees wobble. I took the pink roses that he handed me as we sat down, telling him that should my heart go into somersault mode, it would all be recorded on a memory stick and reported back to the mothership. "Ha," he said, "I have just had a stent replaced and wear those all the time." Then we discussed heart problems and I can report an uneventful graph line, as nothing is quite so far from one's 20-year-old self as a conversation about electrical impulses to the right ventricle. Affairs of the heart at my age are not quite those one remembers from one's youth; heartache takes on an entirely different meaning.

Prudery

Doctors and other health professionals in Anglo-Saxon countries can seem quite prudish to Europeans. My sister lived in France for many years, and on her first gynaecological appointment back in the UK, she was shown into the exam room and told to make herself comfortable. She took off all her clothes and lay down on the bed with her feet in the stirrups, as one does in France. The consultant came in, then backed out in horror, his arm over his eyes, shouting, "Nurse, Nurse, come quickly!" Once his heart rate was back to normal, he explained that he had been expecting to see a new patient decently dressed sitting in the armchair opposite him and that he hadn't seen a naked patient in years. There is a huge and elaborate faff about covering and uncovering small bits at a time, in the name of Patient Dignity. Impatient Indignity would be a much better name for all this "May I have a look at your breast?" nonsense. Of course you may, you are my breast surgeon/oncologist/radiotherapist, how are you expected to do your job if I say no?

I did get an insight into the problem from the doctor's side, though. My daughter has a very pretty radiologist friend who goes round crying "Pants ON, pants ON!!" as many of her (particularly male) patients' anatomical awareness is so sketchy that they want to pull their trousers down even for a kidney scan.

Though she also had a shy 16-year-old boy whose pants she practically had to tug off as he thought the sensor could just be waved over his crotch area…

In our (i.e. patients') defence, it really is tiresome to continuously battle with hospital gowns trailing ribbons and gaps and slits, which cover all the parts that someone needs to look at, and leave bare to the breeze all the parts that they don't, and which then have to go straight in the wash and waste water and soap, when you know perfectly well that you are going to have to take it all off a second later so you can have your breasts scanned. Doctors just don't like to enter rooms and find disrobed patients. As mentioned, they cover their eyes, back off and shout for help. You sigh, close the hospital gown till they approach the scanning bed, then take it off again. "We show respect and courtesy to all our patients" explained a young doctor priggishly to me. "But you are turning me into an object of sex just because I am a woman, despite the fact that I am 60 years old with one lopsided breast and a whole lot of scars. You wouldn't tell a man to cover up his chest when having a chest exam would you? You make me feel that there is something indecent about my readiness to show you my breast, while I am just being efficient and helpful. You are going to end up seeing my breasts anyway, so why not straight away?"

There is never an answer to this, we women just have to battle on with those idiotic hospital gowns that are designed for octopuses, whose ribbons do not match anywhere other than at strangulation level round your neck, and, for those of us with chemo ports, have to be removed anyway for every blood test. It is just not done in Anglo-Saxon countries, so that is that.

***

It is possible I have a lax attitude to decency – it is necessary to survive being married to a slightly eccentric Bavarian. The last time I let him arrange a holiday, which was a long time ago, we ended up in Corsica on the 15th of August because he had found cheap tickets on the 14th August, and my objection that we would never find anywhere to stay was overruled with a lofty "Trust me, Corsica will be empty." Corsica was of course, as any sane person would have known, bursting at the seams, overflowing into the sea and up the mountains.

We spent three nights in a building on the grounds of a hotel that was condemned to be demolished at the end of the season, mostly reserved for the hotel's eastern-European seasonal workers and girls wandering around in the evening with mudpacks on their faces and fluffy slippers. I sent Florian out every day to recce for somewhere else. He returned in triumph on day three, saying he had found a fabulous villa on the beach in an all-inclusive resort with a sports centre. That it turned out to be the nudist resort, chosen by him for the sole reason that it had a PADI dive centre (one that we had all nixed before leaving London), was not worth mentioning. All part of his plan it seemed. My husband enjoyed watching a lovely Polish model having windsurfing lessons and the Bologna nurses' beach ball team practice, and finally beating the children at mini golf, as whenever they were in danger of winning, he would drop his swimming trunks, and this would put them off their strokes. Definitely and literally below the belt, they complained. The children spent their time wandering around disconsolately wrapped in as many clothes as they could find, saying that they were cold, and I investigated how naked men did the grocery shopping with no pockets for their wallets. In case that has also puzzled you, the answer is handbags. I can also tell you that naked men on bicycles are not a pretty sight.

I hung around the sporting end of the beach where the sailing teacher was cool with me keeping a bikini bottom on, and only got into trouble once when, forced by jellyfish from my safe haven to the proper nudist end of the beach, I was confronted by a pot-bellied, middle-aged naked man, purple in the face with anger, shouting at me in Italian (which unfortunately I speak) – "How dare you just walk around with a bikini bottom on? Who do you think you are?? It is completely outrageous, take that bikini off IMMEDIATELY." Like a reverse Aphrodite, I slunk into the sea up to waist level and remained there, cursing my husband for having put me in this ludicrous situation.

Complementary Therapies and Diet

"I wish you would write something about alternative therapies," said Prof E. He hasn't learned to call it "complementary" yet, which is what I have been asked to call it, as it is not an alternative to orthodox treatment but a complement. "It is a billion-dollar industry and people do get led astray."

The main issue for doctors is that there are no controlled trials – where group A, a strictly defined bunch of people (or mice), take the therapy, while another group, known as the control group, identically defined, do not, and then results are compared. In practice, this means that my friend Lucy swears by supplement X or re-purposed drug Y, which she is also taking, while no one knows if her continuing good health is due to X, Y, the fact that her conventional treatment is successful, or that she has given up milk or taken up eating lots of broccoli. This is why oncologists call most of the complementary therapy treatments "anecdotal" and say to you that as long as they don't do you any harm, and the money isn't an issue, go for it, but don't feel that you are missing out if you decide not to.

Big Pharma are not trying to hide proven results from you, there is simply no money in running hugely expensive trials and tests and in the end, only having lemon peel or turmeric root to sell.

Some complementary therapies are under trial anyway, so one suggestion is to wait till the trial results come through. Google chat rooms and Facebook groups are actually rather helpful here – if a critical mass of people on the same drug regime as you all agree that some food supplement or over-the-counter drug helps with side effects, then it is probably worth trying.

Well-meaning friends do sometimes try to guilt you into a diet that they have read is anti-cancer, and this can get surprisingly irritating as you have to either lie and say "Oh, thank you, I have never heard of that, but will now give up coffee/meat/grain/dairy/asparagus/fruit/tomatoes/potatoes and live on Purple Sprouting Kale," or explain why, after reading countless articles making exactly the same claims for the polar opposite diet, you have decided not to listen to any more dietary advice. The supplement box in our household grew so large at a certain point, that I threw it all away with a huge sigh of relief, and started from scratch, building up a new and much reduced essential kit consisting of vitamin D, oil of oregano and linseed oil, this last one only because I had typed 30 by mistake into the online order instead of three, and had a stock of bottles for a couple of years. I no longer have any idea what it is supposed to be good for, sadly.

The Trial Clinic where I am registered did suggest that I get a biome analysis done – a snapshot of your intestinal flora – which is one of the latest areas of oncology research. Dr R, the head of the research clinic, was an earnest young German doctor who specialises in this field, added with disarming humility, "Of course, my wife has been telling me for years that everyone who ever read a popular science and nutrition book knows the importance of this already – it is only we cutting-edge research scientists who don't."

In a radiology corridor, waiting for a scan, I sat opposite a pale, emaciated young woman who looked scared and frail. "Do the scans hurt?" she asked pathetically. I assured her that they didn't, and as she seemed to be a 'new girl,' I asked her how she was finding it.

"I don't want to have chemo," she said, "It is poison and I have a small baby."

"Surely all the more reason to have chemo then," I said gently, "And you are young, you will feel right as rain again in a few months."

"I want to treat it holistically," she said, "I don't want chemo, I am going to eat broccoli sprouts."

I asked her how her partner felt about her refusing chemo. "He doesn't want me to have it either," she said.

I tried to find a bland reply, but all I could come up with was, "Don't let the thought of chemo stress you, as stress is so bad for you, and broccoli sprouts and kale are disgusting." She looked at me with the eyes of a fanatic. "I love kale and broccoli sprouts."

I left it at that but felt a little sorry for her oncologist. Popular science and nutrition books fulfil the same function, I imagine, as popular preachers did in the 16th century; whipping their parishioners into a frenzy with chants and rosaries on how to achieve eternal life, avoid the hellfire and the red-hot poker that is IBS. I would have been as sceptical then as I am now.

The Acupuncturist

"I keep telling you, you must go to my acupuncturist, Dr J – he is simply amazing. I feel so much better. I could hardly walk last week, and now look at me!"

This is what I overheard a well-dressed woman standing outside a shop saying to her friend as I was loitering around waiting to go to chemo. Well of course, I had to touch her arm and say that I was sorry to eavesdrop, but would she mind telling me about this amazing acupuncturist?

"Of course!" she said in surprise, "He is just down the road. Take down my mobile number and I will send you his contact details." "Kind Stranger" is still an entry in my phone. I googled Dr J and read that his father had, to alleviate their suffering, practiced acupuncture on fellow inmates in a POW camp run by the Japanese, and this had inspired Dr J himself to follow in his father's footsteps. I was not sure that it was entirely credible for the Japanese to have allowed acupuncture needles into a POW camp, but it was a good story, and I rang Dr J a few weeks later to see what he could do for my perennially stiff neck and sore shoulder.

I dread the history-taking, because as soon as I mention that I have cancer, which I avoid doing until forced to, people try to look compassionate and understanding, lose all interest in my infected finger or stiff neck or whatever and urge upon me a holistic package including counselling and meditation apps. "I have a stiff neck, and I only mentioned that I have insomnia as it is a well-known side effect of a drug I have to take. I don't want a holistic approach." I say, but it is always in vain.

Dr J started badly by telling me how important it was to treat the whole person; physical and metaphysical. "If you are a machine, we have to look at how the whole engine works, we can't just order a spare part from John Lewis. We need to build up your immune system and support your body's weaknesses so it can heal itself. Then we can look at your neck and shoulder."

This had a whiff of the sales patter that targets vulnerable and anxious women and reminded me of a previous appointment with one of these miracle-working society healers. Paul, we shall call him, had mesmeric blue eyes that goggled meaningfully at you, and he was completely aware of their effect. Kaa, the snake in *The Jungle Book*, had similar eyes. As I lay on what was essentially a vibrating massage bed (Paul not being a great believer in physical exertion), while he emanated healing vibrations at me, he interrupted his emanations to take a phone call from a very distraught sounding female patient. After he hung up, he turned to me and said, tut-tutting:

"Poor lady, I have been seeing her for her allergies for months, and we were finally getting somewhere. I had persuaded her to let me prepare a tincture made of her own urine to build up her immune system, and after a few weeks of this, I was able to diagnose that the chief allergen was in fact her husband, and we needed to make up a tincture of his urine too. It is very frustrating, but the husband has now forbidden her to continue with the sessions. Such a shame." He sighed sorrowfully and swivelled his eyes at me in an intense kind of way, making them as blue as he could. "So, when can you come next week?"

Pushing aside this memory, I turned my attention back to what Dr J was saying about looking deeply into the individual's immune system and weak points. I shuddered to think of the reaction of the Old School Bavarian Gent were he to be told that I was allergic to him, and he had to submit to the urine tincture regime.

To forestall Dr J's next step, which would clearly have been to say that it would take about a year of weekly visits at £120 a pop, I said that, with the greatest respect, I took a different approach: I am a run-down second-hand car with bits falling off and an engine that doesn't bear too much scrutiny. All I want him to do is fix a door that doesn't close and then we will see about the rest which, frankly, as long as the car starts, is good enough for me as that is just the way this car is. Unfixable, there we have it, nothing to be done, and all I really want, is for the door to close and in just a few sessions as well. This is precisely the state of my 15-year-old, blue Toyota Ignis which just scrapes through its MOT every year but still drives down to Waitrose with swagger, and I require nothing more of it than that.

"Ah," said Doctor J in a consciously understanding and musical voice, "I can see just from this brief conversation, without even having met you, what the big picture is. Please give me a chance to look at the whole car." He then went on to ask how I had heard about him. I told him about his little fan club on Marylebone High St. "I pay them to stand there and say how good I am," he said with a snort of laughter, so I booked an appointment. Just the sort of mechanic I need.

As it turned out, the session was a great success. Buddhas smiled fatly and enigmatically down at me from various shelves, and Dr J stuck one needle in my ear, saying "To calm you down". I think he was beginning to see the big picture after all. The next day my shoulder was no better, but the pains in my legs and feet had disappeared completely, so I booked another appointment. After all, at £100, the follow up sessions were a steal.

Other Helpful Tips

I find that I am frequently asked by new arrivals in Cancerland about how to deal with the bewildering plethora of doctors. I have one very good tip: go into each appointment with a piece of paper on which you have written every question that you have wondered about since you last saw the doctor, no matter how silly it seems, plus any links to articles you have read that you want your doctor to comment on. Do nothing until the doctor has explained what he thinks you should know and has started to show signs of wanting to show you the door. At that point, you calmly pull out your list, say "Would you mind if I just asked a few questions that I have prepared since I last saw you?" Then, look at your list, cross out any questions that have been answered or rendered unnecessary, and go over the rest. Your doctor will soon get used to you doing this, you will be able to keep family and friends informed and be far less tempted to google things. Four years on and I still do this. Prof E has developed his own technique of dealing with me, which is to say, "Excellent question," before telling my why it does not apply in my case.

Another good tip is to talk to everyone you can who is looking after you – the nurses, the radiologists, anyone at all, as they will all have different experiences, and by collecting enough mosaic tiles, you will end up with an interesting picture and a broader range of opinions. I have noticed, for example, that the loftier the consultant, the less he or she knows about side effects – they are just not on the radar which is tuned to higher things – and a good thing too of course as they need to focus on the big picture of keeping you alive. However, it is quite nice to be able to moan about flatulence and cramps, constipation and split fingernails to an experienced nurse who has spent years listening to people bang on about these things, as that is what you spend a lot of your day dealing with. Prof E is always so pleased to see me, and says with such evident pleasure, "You are looking so well, I bet you feel really good too!" that out of sheer kindness, I never tell him about the niggles. I hate to be a spoilsport.

***

On the subject of medical tips, there is something extremely important that I want to tell you. Making small talk one day while I was having a scan, the radiologist asked me how I found having a permanently installed chemo-port (a small box inserted into your chest which gives easy access for chemo and avoids people sticking needles into veins). "I love it," I said, "It makes me happy every day that no one is ever going to stick a needle into me again, and in fact, I cannot think why, in this day and age, one still sees people having chemo with needles taped into their arms or hands, it is barbaric..." "Yes," agreed the doctor, "And what is more, it really does destroy your veins and causes all kinds of trouble. The problem is that we are not allowed to recommend inserting a chemo-port, only to suggest it as an option. I have just come from a re-training session, and we have been told that we are never to make personal recommendations about treatment, surgery or anything, as if something goes wrong, we can be sued. We are supposed to list all the options– for example, a surgeon must tell you that you can have a) no

31

surgery, b) a lumpectomy, c) a mastectomy, d) a double mastectomy etc, without influencing the patient one way or another."

I was speechless (well, not literally of course), "What on earth is the point of having a surgeon or oncologist if she is not allowed to influence your decisions?" I asked in indignation. "How are we supposed to know what the best option is?"

"I know," said the doctor, "It is ridiculous, but all we can do is say, if asked, what we would do *if it were us...* that way it is a fact rather than a recommendation."

So, there we are. Always ask your doctor/surgeon/oncologist what they would do if it were them/their wife/their husband. And pass it on.

***

Final tip: Physics. Yes, Quantum Theory, the General Theory of Relativity, Standard Model particle physics, the works, and the more obscure the better. I went to an extremely bad school where maths was for the few brainboxes, and physics and chemistry were taught by dear Mrs Ware, with her frizzy hair escaping in wisps from her hair pins, reading glasses always askew, and a happy knack for blowing things up with Bunsen burners by mistake while we cowered behind the benches, stuffing our regulation hankies in our mouths to stop laughing. We used to ask, partly to wind her up, but also out of interest, "But Mrs Ware, what are molecules made of?" then, "And what are atoms made of, what are neutrons made of, what is matter made of, and what was there before matter, and what is space made of, what is outside of space, and, and, and..."

Eventually Mrs Ware would crack (well, it was 1969, and the answers were still a little hazy), and say, "Right girls, enough of that, get out your test tubes, turn on your Bunsen burner, no, Rosie Pearson, do NOT hide under the bench yet, I want you to watch what I am doing, and let's add a little magnesium sulphate to the hydrochloric acid and then ..." BOOOOOMMMMM.

One of the perks of living a medical life is that you have, if you are interested, the sort of access to and inspiration from clever scientific minds that Mrs Ware's students could only dream of (except for the Christie twins, who went on to become doctors and medical professors, goodness knows how). By far my favourite reading is now physics, from the bizarre, microscopic quantum level stuff to the dreamscape of foaming baby universes which froth up, pop and disappear like bubbles in a bubble bath. This, I think, has armed me with an equanimity and slightly amused detachment in the face of everything from petty irritations like cramps at night, to the timing of one's personal extinction, and indeed that of the human race. As Arthur C. Clarke wrote, "The time was fast approaching when Earth, like all mothers, must say farewell to her children."

I would just point out that Earth is apparently not a Jewish-Greek mother – who does not let go of her children *ever* – but on the whole, Arthur is right, and I can no longer get worked up about anything much at all.

My tip is to buy the book that started me off on my own space odyssey: *The Universe in Your Hand* by Christophe Galfard. My personal wormhole to a fabulous parallel universe.

"Good morning Dr Chandra, this is Hal, I am ready for my first lesson."

This is also an excellent tip for insomnia. Not that books about physics are boring, far from it – they are uniformly beautifully written and real page turners (I mean, we are talking about the highest stakes that exist here) – but after turning two pages, one's poor brain is so tired from the effort of understanding and digesting, that a third page often remains unread, and sleep takes over.

Snowflakes in Cancerland

I tried very hard not to feel insulted when my oncologist wrote in one of his post-clinic reports, cc'd to anyone who has ever seen me or my breast, "Ileana has an indolent cancer." How very rude, I thought. As a friend of mine wrote, "It really is time you ended this relationship with your C. You have such different personalities..."

I wrote a letter to Prof E on behalf of my "C" complaining about his insensitivity and offensive language; he could have called it shy, timid, docile, well-bred, undemanding, tranquil, chilled, relaxed, quiet, discreet, modest, but *indolent??* I got a swift reply from his secretary, yellow- highlighting the relevant interpretation for me to make sure no further offence was caused.

"Thank you for your letter. I feel I should try and explain what is meant by indolent in this setting.

Indolent metastatic breast cancer is a clinical term and is used frequently to describe a tumour that is not growing/growing slowly.

In one sense, indolent means lazy, lethargic, or idle, being averse to activity or movement.

When applied to a medical situation, indolent can mean a problem that causes no pain, or is slow-growing and not immediately problematic.

Prof E. certainly didn't mean to offend "your C" by writing that in his letter and I'm sorry that he did."

Well, it was a Friday afternoon, not peak sense of humour time. However, when doctors feel that they aren't allowed to offend a cancer cell, you know that the pendulum has swung a bit too far…

The Dermatologist

Melanomas do not run in my family, so I am not very skin aware, but one day I noticed a large and bleeding mole and was duly sent off to see the dermatologist. Docteur de la P was a very smart French lady in an immaculate suit, perfectly coiffed and manicured. She looked over my whole body with a magnifying camera and found nothing, until she looked between my toes – apparently a favourite hiding place for melanomas. "Oh la la, what 'ave we 'ere!" she exclaimed, then reached for her scalpel saying, "Zees might 'urt…" It didn't hurt, and on inspection, it turned out to be a bit of old sock-fluff… utterly mortifying. She then looked at the soles of my feet and said "We seem to 'ave a lot of zings embedded in 'ere..." The "We" was a kindness of course. I said weakly that I had had a bath the night before but had been on a walking holiday. "Better zan a melanoma" she said cheerfully, and carefully removed all the bits of old sock fluff and gravel and whatever else she found. I now have a digital map of all the moles and odds and ends embedded in my skin.

Letting Yourself Go

I may have to go and see Docteur de la P again sometime, so a little pulling of myself together might be in order. Greek women are always incredibly well-groomed and their beauty routines make English un-lifted jaws drop (even further) in disbelief. I was once frog-marched off by a Greek cousin to her hairdresser in Athens, as I was clearly looking unkempt. Five and a half hours later, after my hair had been washed, cut and dried no less than three times by two different people, and I had heard the gossip of *le tout Athenes* about whose beautifully coiffed and highlighted wife was sleeping with whose philandering husband, I was then offered "the full *maquillage*". I refused in a panic, fearing that I would never escape, and fled before they could stop me. The next day I left for our small Greek island, and, happily walking across the hills through the silvery olive trees with the fresh wind blowing through my (very groomed) hair, an old crone in black, perched like a crow in an olive tree where she was picking olives, called down to me; "Hey, you boy, who are you and where are you going?"

I replied with my name and said I was just going home... "Oh, it's you, I didn't recognise you. I thought you were an *alvanaki*" (the word for the peasant boys who used to come down from Albania at olive-picking season, and were unjustly regarded with great suspicion by locals). I complained to my cousin about this – after having spent *five hours* at the chicest hairdresser in Athens. "Well, what did you expect?" she said crossly, "You didn't have the full *maquillage*. Of course you look like an Albanian peasant boy."

A few weeks ago, she and her sister took me out for dinner, and as we sat down, she said to me severely, "Ileana, you are looking wrinkled. Just because you have cancer, there is no reason to let yourself go. You should be moisturising with collagen masks, and what you need is a little Botox *here*, a little filler *here*, and of course, you should have strings put into your cheeks to hold up your jawline."

"What??" I said incredulously.

"Oh, come on," she said a trifle impatiently, "You know what I mean, I am sure that all your friends have already done it, they just don't tell you." Her sister nodded in agreement. Cancerland is not the only parallel planet out there.

These cousins are strong, clever, independent women with their heads screwed on and their feet on the ground, but one of them, following what she claims to be nightly visitations from aliens, believes that extra-terrestrials from the Pleiades constellation planted their seed into a few select humans eons ago, and that these aliens make contact with us every now and then to nudge us, their disappointing and self-destructing descendants, back onto the right path from which we have strayed while under the evil influence of Giant Lizards. The other cousin nods in sisterly understanding as this is explained to me. As I said, there are many parallel planets on which people reside. Cancerland is just one of them, and by no means the strangest.

Still, some things have to be taken seriously, so when I got back to London, I not only spent a small fortune on minute pots of face creams, but also made an appointment at the hairdresser – for the first time in three years, as my home-dyeing of my nice new post-chemo hair with organic, natural colour had only been partially successful. At least twice a week, people would say to me how cool it was that someone of my age had chosen to have purple hair. The hairdresser nodded when I told her that and added that the band of green around the ends could also go. I now look almost groomed enough for my Athenian cousins.

Ageing

Ageing takes on a very different aspect when your health is compromised; getting older is a goal, and not something to be ashamed of. When I hit 60, my friend Emma threw me a birthday party. It took several goes to organise as chemo tends to accelerate the usual cognitive decline. The invitation that finally got sent out had to be immediately corrected with another missive:

"The secret of our long and happy marriage is that Florian and I never talk to each other, so when I told him the date for my birthday party, his reply via email was "I can't make it, I will be in Germany." As I know it will be more fun with him there, Emma and I would like to move the party to Monday 21st October, and hope that you can still make it. Emma, who is a saint, has assured me that everyone expects anything to do with my family to be chaotic, so it is not at all embarrassing."

And then, the Lawyer son's training in the careful reading of all documents resulted in him sending one more amendment:

"Whilst it would be befitting of our family chaos for people to turn up on different days, I should perhaps point out that the Monday is the 22nd rather than the 21st..."

Amazingly, all my 60-something-year-old friends managed to turn up on the right day, as did Florian and I.

"How brave of you to admit to 60, I am sure I will never do that, I will just hide and pretend it isn't happening," said my friend Nicola with all the smugness of a beautiful 59-year-old. "I am thrilled to be 60," I replied, "The alternative is dying at 59, and from now on, I will announce every year I get older, and expect cards and presents." "Oh, how insensitive of me," she cried to my great satisfaction, and came to the party with a suitably beautiful and golden birthday present which I wear at every possible occasion.

The next year, she had learned her lesson, and called me two days before my birthday. "I just wanted to congratulate you on making it to 61," she said. "I know that in your case, getting old is a good thing and you cannot take it for granted that you will always make it another year, so congratulations."

"Oh," I said, trying very hard not to laugh, "That is so sweet of you, but Nicola, that applies to everyone, you might get hit by a bus tomorrow and not make it to your next birthday either!"

Nicola wasn't having any of that. "You know what I mean, you have a serious health problem and I don't."

She was quite right of course, and I did know what she meant. "Well, I think to be honest, the person we probably ought to be congratulating on my birthdays from now on is Prof E. Perhaps my friends could club together and buy him a case of Champagne every year that I make it?"

"Champagne?" cracked back the reply like a whip, "What makes you think we love you that much?"

"Fine," I said, "Prosecco then."

Sorry, Prof, I tried.

Embracing ageing does not mean that I am devoid of vanity or above a little flattery; my cardiologist recently prescribed some new pills for my huffing and puffing, which he said were taken by millions of old people with no ill effects at all. He saw my face, and added hastily, "But I am giving you a paediatric dose that I prescribe for small children." I made sure to bring this to the pharmacist's attention as I handed over the prescription, just in case he thought I was an old person…

Dr L is not only sensitive and warm-hearted, he is also unbelievably humble. At my last appointment with him, one of those scenarios unfolded about which one fantasises, but one knows will clearly never happen. While sitting in his waiting room reading the *Daily Mail*, I came across an article hyperventilating with excitement over the promising test results of using Metformin, a cheap drug for diabetics, to mitigate the heart problems and huffing and puffing caused by my type of treatment, which is the side effect that makes you feel really old and decrepit.

I mentioned this diffidently to Dr L using all the approved formulae ("I am sure you are following this and have already decided that it is not appropriate, but I wondered if you had had a chance to see the *Daily Mail* on Metformin today?"). Usually this elicits a sigh and some eye-rolling from your consultant or doctor, but Dr L is young and cool, and said with interest, "No, actually I haven't, I would I love to read that." Doctors never say this, ever. I cannot begin to describe how unusual this is.

"Don't move," I said before he could retract this bombshell, leaping to my feet and charging out to the waiting room. I snatched the newspaper and brought it back with me, totally out of breath with the sudden exertion. Dr L scanned it and then said, "That is so interesting, if you want to try it, I approve. Talk to your GP."

Literally two days after taking it, my huffing and puffing stopped, I could run upstairs pushing elderly people and push-chair-toting mothers out of the way as in my heyday, and I felt my usual age again.

***

While feeling 60 rather than 80 is nice, it remains my view that ageing has its hidden pleasures of which the young are unaware. Stem cell research, telomere extensions and fasting for 22 hours a day are just some of the keys to eternal life that are being researched on mice in Californian laboratories (and even on some Silicon Valley millionaires who haven't really thought it through), but the searchers for eternal youth are missing out on the joys of winding down, not taking things seriously, forgetting and giving in to sloth and distraction. Getting older can be the greatest self-indulgence that there is – a closely guarded secret. Don't tell the young ones.

A typical conversation as an uninhibited older person that I recently had with my older sister Marina went as follows.

Marina: "Shall we watch something on TV?"

Me: "Yes, I seem to have taped something called *Succession*. No idea what it is, some sort of US box series – or perhaps I didn't tape it and someone else did. I can't remember."

Marina: "OK, let's try that."

After five minutes…

Marina: "This is really boring – no one says those sorts of things or carries on like that in real life."

Me: "Perhaps they do, perhaps they don't, but the thing is, I can't understand anything they say – they quack like ducks, quack-quack-quack – not a single word."

Marina: "It doesn't matter if you don't understand, as what they say is rubbish, no one carries on like that in real life."

Me: "Even if it weren't rubbish, even if it were Einstein on the General Theory of Relativity, I still can't understand what they say, they all quack like ducks."

Marina: "you don't need to understand, it is all rubbish."

Me: "But even if it weren't rubbish, I don't understand a word they say, it is all quack- quack-qu…"

Marina, cracking first, "Let's go and have a snack instead."

Me: "Good idea, I might have a bath too."

We go into the kitchen and look at the old Babar the Elephant clock with the ticking legs that hasn't needed a new battery since 1992.

Marina: "Oh my God, do you really think that no one has put a battery in since 1992?" Cracks up…

Me: "Oh goody, according to Babar, it is 7 o'clock already, I can have a snack, then a bath and go to bed."

We both dissolve into laughter and then have to run for the nearest loo.

***

I am also showing signs of the increasing lack of inhibition that joyfully accompanies getting older. An old friend with his new wife had come for dinner, and he was filling her in on some of his more colourful family members and their stories.

"Great Uncle Giovanni was of course a disreputable figure, who lived a very dissolute life – girlfriends, financial scandals, family schisms, fights over wills – the works. He was very well known in Italy. On top of that, he died in a suspicious way, and everyone thought it was his wife who had murdered him for his money so she could take a younger lover."

"How did he die?" we all asked curiously.

"He died in his bath, electrocuted by inexplicably faulty wiring. The papers were full of it for days. Of course, it was a terrible shock."

I just howled with laughter and everyone stared aghast at me.

"Electrocuted in his bath, a terrible shock…"

The staring continued.

"Electric shock, everyone shocked, geddit?"

They didn't get it, or if they did, they didn't think it was funny. Not even a polite smile, just consternation at my appalling manners. I subsided into silence.

Multi-tasking is admittedly not as easy as it used to be. The usual victim of memory deficit is anything I am cooking. I put asparagus on the hob for a quick five-minute steam, then go upstairs to write a short email, see an unpaid invoice, log on to my online banking, find that my password has been compromised, have to reset it, which means dealing with being unable to remember my security questions, put all that aside as it is too dull, start to go down for a cup of tea, remember that I didn't send that email, and so on, until 45 minutes later, I hear plaintive calls from Florian asking me what is burning in the kitchen. I have charred beyond redemption more saucepans than I like to remember (or can remember to be honest), and the kitchen has a permanent whiff of smoke. A recent home-made, garden-foraging pie with a delicious filling of dandelions, sorrel, spinach, nettles and a few accidental bits and bobs survived two burnings thanks to Florian's intervention, and he sat me down for stern pep talk. "I understand that you have to juggle work and cooking, but you are clearly getting too old to be trusted to do more than one thing at a time."

"I know," I said meekly, "That is why I need to retire soon so I can focus on cooking for you."

Florian surveyed the garden-foraging pie with a notable lack of enthusiasm and then said,

"Better keep working and forget about the cooking."

I do sometimes worry that I am overly embracing the whole ageing thing. Once the novelty wears off, I might have to do something about it, but until then, it is so much fun.

Bumps in the Road

It slowly dawned on me that being in remission actually means dealing with the side effects of drugs rather than with cancer. I must remember to feel grateful for this, while also remembering that no one has any remedies for these annoyances – other than more drugs with more side effects, so in the end you take stinging nettle powder, and any other mumbo-jumbo you can think of, hoping that there is at least some science behind the placebo effect if not behind stinging nettle powder...

The feeling grateful can sometimes be a bit hard, but it was suddenly made a lot easier when one of my routine test results came back less than ideal (not a fail, but definitely a "could you please see me in my office after the class has left" ...)

Prof E was uncharacteristically beating around the bush and getting irritated at my trying to flush him out. Subordinate clauses were tangled up in the branches, trapped metaphors beating their wings weakly trying to escape the thorns. But a bush can only take so much beating, and eventually I managed to get him out into the daylight. "Minor alerts in the lymph nodes under your stomach and a larger one in your neck. Your tumour markers aren't showing anything, which is good, but we must get these biopsied." My C was no longer indolent. It was back.

I had a careful, Proustian look at the emotions that arose when hearing that my disease had probably progressed. A couple of tears squeezed themselves out and down my cheeks, and Prof E pushed his large Kleenex box towards me. I wondered how long it would take me to find the positive in all this, for Pollyanna to appear with her duster, for the Baby Chamois to bound across my screen.

The first transforming ray of sunshine appeared as Prof E said the magic words "Trial clinic". That, as we know, is for Special People with interesting diseases, not for the hoi polloi, and a warm glow of gratification started to spread over me. "Can we try your new drug, those little nuclear bombs that you told me about last year, the ones that are front loaded with targeted chemo and with smart guided controls, that you keep in your box of magic tricks for advanced students?" I asked him.

"Yes, of course, my T-DM1s are just perfect for that, and you always wanted to play with them, so now we can."

Pollyanna needs, as it turns out, about 45 minutes to get to work. Before going into Prof E's room, I had noticed a new nurse whose function there was not clear to me and to whom I had paid no attention at first. Now, as I left Prof E's room, with his arm comfortingly around my shoulder, and me still blowing my nose and mopping up a few tears, he propelled me into her care and said, "She will now look after you." She didn't seem to need any briefing, so I asked her if she had been sent up specially in case I needed counselling (which I had been skilfully and successfully dodging for three years now, as Prof E knew perfectly well...)

"I am here to offer support," she said, with no idea of the thinness of the ice upon which she was skating.

"So you have a list of patients who are due to get bad news, and then you nip upstairs and pounce on them?" I asked, "If so, you are, in a sense, the Grim Reaper's representative – the *Angel of Death* – where you appear, Death cannot be far behind...."

"Oh, no," she said, goggling with disapproval and alarm at me, "I prefer to think of myself just as an angel."

She then peered earnestly into my eyes and said in a low, intense voice full of sympathy, "THERE IS ALWAYS HOPE."

This was the point where I understood that one must never let anyone else control the narrative. The Angel of Death's line, that she had nothing to offer except hope, was not one I was going to like at all. *And this is where my storytelling practice, my Narratotherapy of the last few years paid off.* I tried out in my mind a couple of versions, none of which used the word "hope" at all. In fact, the word "hope", when uttered by the medical profession, is to my mind like the last rites. Hope is when all else has failed, and as I know that Prof E still has a whole arsenal of exciting toys to pull out of his toy chest, I am nowhere near needing hope. So, the narrating part of my brain got to work, and by the time the Tuesday Lunch Club had turned up for that day's clinic lunch, I had run through and discarded a few versions, flipped a few trial pancakes, and cheerfully told them that this current, unbelievable run of luck had come to an end, and we should all expect there to be bumps in the road. "We can't panic every time a few cancer cells wake up," is what my Pollyanna

43

Personality Disorder came up with, "First of all, it is such early days that Prof E can't even be sure, then, if it does turn out to be cancer cells, he is going to smoke them out, cut off their supplies and then blast them with all sorts of brand-new goodies,". After that, there were no more tears and that was the end of that.

Back at the trial clinic for VIPs, which I now was again, it was time for some lessons in molecular biology. Dr A, who certainly flunked his art classes, drew some rather wobbly and scratchy diagrams of how we would stop malicious software from attaching itself to the surface of the cancer cells and signalling "Go forth and multiply!" messages, while blowing the cells up from the inside with Prof E's T-DM1s. I felt like General Petraeus with a map of Tora Bora... my poor, indolent C was going to be in serious trouble here. I almost felt sorry for it.

"We will give it another couple of months," said Prof E, "As there is really not quite enough evidence of anything yet, nothing big enough to biopsy, and then we will rescan you after that, see if it looks any clearer, and decide what to do."

When Not to Be Brave

There are certain things that put a little cancer into perspective; and the foremost among these is toothache.

A week after my visit to Prof E, I felt with some pride that I had got the hang of things. What I had not got the hang of was a dental abscess, which burst upon me with unprecedented vigour and in both upper and lower jaw.

In excruciating pain and rattling with antibiotics, painkillers and sleeping pills – I cried. For six days and nights I snivelled and moaned and keened and wept. I sat on my bed and wailed, I watched hours of MGM musicals with tears running down my cheeks, I bawled my eyes out, I sobbed and blubbed and howled like a wolf. Even *I* was embarrassed at myself, to say nothing of my heroic dentist who had incautiously given me his mobile number and to whom I sent hourly updates of how swollen my face was. Danae tried to cheer me up by posting a photo of Marlon Brando in his Godfather days with his cheeks padded out, onto our office WhatsApp group. It made the office laugh, anyway.

The upside of course, as I said to the dentist a few days later as he proclaimed the abscess shrunk enough to pull out two teeth, was that it probably explained the alarmingly lit-up lymph node that my last PET scan had showed – the one that had Prof E looking worried and talking about trial clinics again, and the Angel of Death hovering in the wings. No one had ever been so happy to hear that they had had the mother of all abscesses requiring two teeth to be pulled out. Sitting in a happy, sedated and blissfully pain-free haze in the dentist chair, I gave my dentist a huge and bloody smile that went from ear to ear. (Well, not quite from ear to ear as half my face was blown up like a balloon and wasn't moving at all, but he got the message.)

There will be no more false modesty now when I say to people who tell me how brave and strong I am, "Oh, no, I am *really* not brave at all, you should see me with toothache." In my defence, the time to indulge in riptides of self-pity, is when you know that something is going to pass, an end is in sight and no one will worry if you fall apart.

As it turned out, three months after the tooth abscess, the scans still showed the lymph nodes lit up and rather bigger, meaning the tooth abscess was not the cause and it was indeed some pesky cancer cells waking up and stretching. I couldn't decide whether the prospect of returning to downtown Cancerland from the leafy residential quarter of Remission was like coming back to work after a long holiday, or else the beginning of a rather welcome semi-retirement to a Cancerland filled with love and friendship, where other things really aren't valued so highly. The main headache is keeping those around you from panicking. One useful tip is to talk of "cancer cells" rather than "cancer", as this focuses on small targets that can be physically zapped, rather than a vague ectoplasm of a malevolent demon… It has certainly helped me at any rate.

The Biopsy

The lymph nodes were small and in places that were tricky to reach, so it was hard to get a sample of tissue or biopsy to enable Prof E to choose which of his drugs he wanted to play with. Doctor Number 1 gave up pretty fast, and after a wait of a couple of months for the nodes to grow a bit, Doctor Number 2 was consulted, pronounced herself satisfied that she could do it, and I was duly booked in for the biopsy. The door to my hospital room where I was waiting to be prepped for the procedure opened, and in came a Diane Keaton lookalike. "Hello, I am Dr G," she said, shaking hands and looking at me blankly as I fumbled to turn off my iPad, whose buttons continue to baffle me even when not in stressful situations. "I am so sorry," I apologised, "I am not very good at this." Embarrassingly it was showing a very tasteful lesbian scene from the excellent French Netflix comedy "Call my Agent" All very gallic and chic, if a little loud. She stared at me in a rather disconcerting way, and there was an awkward silence, which are things I always feel stupidly obliged to fill, so I complimented her on her tan. She looked down at her hands and said, "Florida. You can't avoid getting a tan in Florida." There was then a long pause while she continued to look at me blankly. "There are a lot of orange people in Florida. Very orange. Lots of them." This time, I just sat there weakly and waited for the next awkward pause to end. It did eventually, with her outlining what she was proposing to do and asking if I agreed and would sign the consent form. "If you don't," she said, "We can all go and have lunch." She sounded serious. I assured her that I wanted to go through with it and could wait for lunch, so after one more awkward silence, she left the room. Surgeons are a strange race, no one as empathetic as George Clooney would have made it in the real world of surgery, where a meticulous attention to detail and a total lack of interest in the big picture seems to be the *sine qua non* of success. The nurses agreed that they had never come across a George Clooney and many surgeons were on the eccentric side. "You can tell from the footsteps when they come down the corridor if it is a surgeon or not," one whispered to me.

46

The biopsy was not a fun one. You lie on your side in a scanner while Dr G sits unseen and silently behind your back and administers local anaesthetic, pokes, pulls, pushes, and you have no idea what is happening. All the while you slide in and out of the scanner. "Take a deep breath" says the machine, "Exhale", "Take a deep breath", "Exhale", which reminded me irresistibly of the radiation treatment days where the thought of messing up the breathing brought on panic breathing. The thought of panic breathing was enough to trigger it, and I started to hyperventilate – great, heaving breaths, deeper and deeper – while tears rolled down my cheeks and I wished I were somewhere else, hoping all the while that Dr G was not trying to guide a needle between my ribs. I heard a sigh behind me, and her voice saying, "Can you just breathe normally please?" "I am having a panic attack," I sobbed back angrily, "and telling me to breathe normally does not help!"

"Oh!" she exclaimed, "I wondered what was happening. How interesting. Why are you having a panic attack?"

"Because I know I mustn't, that's why", I said.

Dr G came round to where I could see her and peered curiously into my face, then she started to laugh, "That is so funny!" Of course I started to laugh as well, and that was the end of the panic attack and all went smoothly and quickly. "Was it difficult to get to?" I asked, "No," she replied, "Not after you lay still."

I think Dr G has stumbled on the best panic-attack remedy I have ever come across- total lack of sympathy, no offer of counselling, and a hearty laugh.

Mind you, I nearly gave her a panic attack in return when, unsure of the etiquette, I asked if I could say thank you and goodbye after she had retired behind the glass partition to process the results. The nurse beckoned to her to come out, I said my heartfelt thank yous and sorrys. Dr G looked as startled as a rabbit in headlights and bounded back as soon as she could to the safety of her screen. Clearly a brilliant surgeon.

About a year later, I realised that in mentioning the enigmatic orange men of Florida, she had probably meant Trump. If not, I still have no idea what that was about.

Blowing in the Wind

The temptation to google 'what is the life expectancy for ....' followed by the details of your newest development, is always there, like an iced bun that you know will make you feel sick, but is within reach and no one is looking... or an itch that you know will bleed and hurt if you scratch it, but is so itchy... The cream for your itch is to remember that you are a glass half-full kind of person, and that the minute you get up, (these thoughts are usually while lying in bed in the morning), life takes over again and mortality prognoses are an irrelevant waste of time. You know that any sad or bad moment you have is a passing cloud that you can hasten on its way with a strong gust of wind. Feeling happy is my gulf stream so to speak, my prevailing wind, and things go wrong when it veers off course, so you have to take all the right actions to keep it in its proper climactic place. A hugely important tool to control your personal climate is language – finding positive words and messages to focus on and to share with other people – that is why calling it cancer cells rather than cancer is a good idea, why I avoid counselling and why laughter cuts through panic attacks so well. You choose good things on which to concentrate, and watch clouds recede over the horizon.

A while ago, one of my children conducted a personality test on the family, where you are asked to imagine a scenario set in an empty desert; a neutral background, and then to flesh out details, where the choices you make illuminate your personality – as interpreted by your child. One of the instructions was to imagine a storm. My storm was a teeny-weeny, dark grey cartoon cloud sailing off stage-left at a good pace, with a few lightning flashes streaking out of it, while the sun continued to shine on the main scene. According to the invigilating daughter, the storm represented troubles in your life, so in other words, I am hardwired to reduce to the smallest possible dimension anything upsetting. I would have passed the personality test with flying colours had I not also imagined the flowers; My house (self) was open and warm and friendly and specifically, always full of food. My horse (husband) was never tethered or fenced in, but stood loyally nearby waiting to be of use. My goats (friends) grazed happily around me. Then I was told to imagine the flowers.

"What flowers?" I complained, suddenly and inexplicably irritated, "We are in a desert here, there is no water, who would be stupid enough to try to grow flowers?" "Just imagine them and stop grumbling," ordered the commanding child. I bad-temperedly imagined an awkward bunch of yellow dahlias, my least favourite flowers, tied with string and wrapped in plastic, an unwelcome gift from a cheap petrol station store, lying in front of my house. "What a nuisance" I muttered, "Now I will have to find a vase, bring them inside and remember to water them, and I hate yellow dahlias."

The flowers are, as my daughter then reproachfully explained to me, your children. "Look on the bright side," I said, "I didn't leave the flowers out to die or throw them away, I did in fact bring them in and put them in water…" Personality tests have their limitations, and interestingly, they don't work at all on Old School Bavarian Gents:

"Daddy, imagine you are in a desert."
"Which desert?"
"It doesn't matter which, say the Sahara Desert."
"But why would I be in the Sahara Desert?
"OK, say the Atacama."
"But I don't want to be in a desert, I would rather be in a forest."
"You can't be in a forest. It has to be a desert."
"I will only play if I can be in a forest, I want trees."
"OK, you are in a forest. Now, imagine your house."
"What sort of house?"
"Any sort, don't overthink it, just imagine a house."
Uncomfortable silence for a few minutes with the Old School Bavarian Gent wrinkling his forehead in unhappiness.
"I don't understand, how can I imagine a house without knowing what sort of house?"
"It can be any kind of house; a Schloss, a tree house, whatever you like, just imagine something."
Another silence.
"I still don't understand."
"Daddy, do you want to do this test or not?"
"Not."

Not altogether a bad thing as, knowing Florian, the flowers would certainly have been meadow upon meadow of wildflowers scattered every which way. The children would have had a field day with that, so to speak.

Round Four

It took a while, but my gulf stream returned to its customary course, and I was soon able to boast in all sincerity to friends and family that Prof E's preferred replacement treatment, his beloved mini-nuclear bombs, T-DM1s, were a great new development and I was lucky to qualify for them, as opposed to the poor people who were still stuck on boring old Herceptin. T-DM1s are the brand new and shiny *nec plus ultra* of cancer care, and are only available to especially lucky people like me who have gone through the ordinary stuff but still need more. No short cuts are allowed.

They work in a very clever way and are a combination of two drugs. Drug A, Herceptin, identifies my type of cancer cells, which have very special crescent shaped tentacles, or "receptors", which are the ones that cry out "Multiply, multiply!" Herceptin is specially shaped to fit like a key in a lock on to these receptors to block them so that they can't send any signals at all. As this seemed to have stopped working for me, in my new treatment the Herceptin is also booby trapped with Drug B, a drop of highly toxic chemo that can only be administered in microscopic quantities. Once the T-DM1 locks onto the cancer cell, the chemo drop slithers into the cell and then blows it up from inside, hopefully leaving your new hair and fingernails unaffected. Rather poetically, given that I come from the Greek island of Ithaca, home of Odysseus, I see this as a mini Trojan War, which was won by Odysseus after a long and unsuccessful siege by similar stealth, treachery and ingenuity: the Greeks, led by Odysseus, built a giant horse, filled it with armed warriors, and tricked the Trojans into wheeling it into their citadel, whereupon, the armed warriors leapt out, opened the gates of

Troy to the Greeks, and it was all over for the Trojans. In a nice modern twist, with T-DM1s, the armed warriors inside the Herceptin (or should we call it Horseptin?), are wearing suicide vests to make sure the detonation is huge and precisely targeted.

Signing all the consent forms for the new treatment with Prof E was a very relaxing affair. He scanned over the possible side effects saying, "Liver failure, yes, a bit of hepatitis now and then, low white blood cells, low platelet count, neuropathy, itchy palms, cramps, anaemia, heart failure, yada yada, bla bla, nose bleeds, dizzy spells, nausea, blurry eyesight, bla bla, you know all this, all the usual stuff, sign here." I did.

What he didn't mention was hair-loss. Had he done so I may well not have signed.

The morning of my first treatment, I was fine about all the above conditions, but when the nurse at the clinic handed me a leaflet outlining the full list of drug side effects, including hair loss ("hair loss is usually not total, just partial, do not brush, comb, wash, blow dry or dye any remaining hair"), to everyone's surprise, I started crying.

"I didn't realise I was having chemo again," I whispered with tears trickling down my cheeks, "I thought I was having *treatment...*"

Hair loss is not a problem when you know it is coming back again at the end of treatment, but there was no end of treatment this time, and my hair had only just got back to the state where I could blow-dry it and swish it around. Crying is a rookie error though, as tears set off the protocol that ends with a specialist Oncology Support Nurse being summoned to offer you Counselling, when you don't need Counselling, you need a cousin on the phone to say to you, "Don't be so silly, you have plenty of hair, and anyway, if you are not supposed to dye it, blow-dry it, wash it, comb it or tie it back, to be honest, in this climate, the less hair you have the better." Luckily I have one of those cousins, so tears dried up, smiles returned, Specialist Oncology Support Nurses were cancelled, the nurse said, "I haven't ever had anyone lose hair on this treatment, I think they write that on ALL their drug information leaflets," The nice lady opposite came over to sit with me, said she had been coming to the clinic for 25 years and was onto her fifth lot of hair loss. She had got so used to it that the other day, she was in a restaurant when a whole clump of hair fell onto the table as the waiter was serving her soup. He stared at her in horror, she just said, "Bad hair day," smiled sweetly, picked up her spoon and went on eating.

Side Effects

A phony "Arab Spring" follows your first T-DM1 treatment, which is fuelled by steroids given as pre-meds. The steroids make you feel like a gold medal Soviet-era female weight-lifter – you re-organise the sock-drawers, move furniture, mend the vacuum cleaner, bake pies, de-worm the dogs, juice three bushels of kale, weed the garden, chop wood, wash the windows, sack your accountants, install your new router, re-file the emails in your inbox, give yourself a manicure, and it is still only 11.30 in the morning… Then, as in Egypt, after two days, the tanks move into Tahrir Square, and reality takes over. You feel like calling your oncologist to complain that his shiny new T-DM1s are nothing but chemo in sheep's clothing and you want more steroids, and lots of them. But you know how the conversation will go:

You: Prof, I am feeling horrid, I ache all over.

Prof: Ah, yes… some people do feel like that it appears.

You: On top of that, I feel sick all the time, my head is spinning, and I have no appetite other than for chocolate cake which the food police at home won't let me eat.

Prof: Hmm... have you tried taking paracetamol?

You: Prof… please, I am not a complete beginner here, I hope you aren't going to suggest Counselling next, or leaflets…

Prof (looking shifty): No, of course not…

You: What is more, I can't sleep, I have run out of Netflix series, my heart is pounding, I have come out in a rash, and my brain is in a total fug; and I spent half of today wondering if one third of every month is the same as one third of a year, or one third of time in general… and I still can't do the numbers!

Prof: ???

You (patiently): if you feel awful for one third of every month (assuming that one of every three weeks is the same as one third of a month, which it may not be), how much of your life is spent feeling awful? Is it one third? I went to a very bad school and can't do mental arithmetic or any kind of arithmetic to be honest. I asked a friend who was at the same bad school as me, and she just asked if I meant lunar months, so that was no help at all, and I still don't know how much of my life will be spent feeling like this.

Prof (who has had enough of this nonsense by now): So tell me, is the quality of your life acceptable?

You: Yes, it is.

Prof: And do you want to stop the treatment?

You (horrified): No! Good God no!

Prof: Good! Then see you in six weeks' time.

There is only one thing for it, and that is to reach out to social media. You post a picture of yourself looking brave on Facebook, and spend the day surfing the wave of love and biceps, hearts, balloons, thumbs ups and "you can do it's that roll in. The best was a message from a Greek friend who wrote, "I hope it is all over soon!" I know she meant the chemo, but it warranted a whole row of crying-with-laughter emojis. A pink Neraida Freiman turban was a marvellous gift from my thoughtful friend Elizabeth who has a hat shop and can take a gentle hint when she gets it, "I may well lose my hair again and I remember you had a lovely pink Neraida Freiman turban in stock last season that didn't get sold…". I sent her a photo of me wearing it with a big grin on my face and a few carefully arranged wisps of hair peeking out. She sent me by return a photo of an impossibly glossy, flawlessly made-up supermodel, from the cover of a magazine, casually lounging against a column and wearing the turban, pink silk pyjamas and a pout. I still think I wore it better. I mean, if you look like a supermodel, and are the lucky possessor of both hair, eyelashes, eyebrows *and* a pink Neraida Freiman turban which you have just for fun and not because you are trying to hide bald patches, you should be jumping up and down with excitement, not propping up a column and pouting. The girl looks lovely, but someone needs to take her aside and explain a few things to her...

Prof E did introduce me to Hélène, a French patient of his on the same trajectory as I am. I rang her one morning, and she assured me that the beginning can be a bit hard, that it would all be better and that she hardly noticed it anymore. We arranged to meet for coffee. Just from her voice I could tell that she was gentle, graceful, wise, had exquisite manners, delicacy of feeling, not a single attention-seeking bone in her body, and was far too considerate, self-effacing and well-bred to make a fuss over silly things like side effects. No wonder Prof E had said to me, "She is the ideal person for you to meet." I resolved on the spot to be gentle, delicate, self-effacing and better-bred and not whine any more. Game, set and match to Prof E, and probably not a huge loss to literature either. Ha, said my children, let's see how long that lasts.

Pollyanna Goes AWOL

It was alarming to see how quickly things deteriorate when you get behind on the psychic housekeeping. My pearl, Pollyanna, just when I needed her most to cope with the disappointing response to Prof E's T-DM1 drugs, was not her usual cheerful self. She was having an off-day, or rather an off-couple-of-months to be more precise. In fact, if I am being frank, she had gone totally AWOL... After a few months of the T-DM1 treatment, she just stopped turning up to work at all. Out of the 21 days between treatments, two were steroid fuelled highs, three were proper write-offs and then over a week was spent getting it back together again, leaving just over a week of quality time. Aches and pains, fevers and fatigue – the works. Scheduling travel, meetings and work days all became a nightmare. I started to do what I swore I would never do, namely, whinge. After a month of this, I could see that the effect of my whinging on my nearest and dearest was not good, so I finally resolved to pull myself together.

Me: OK, so Pollyanna, where the hell are you? Why is my glass no longer half full but half empty? Why am I no longer able to feel lucky to be where I am? Why am I on the verge of thinking "why me?"

Pollyanna: Well, if you think about it, you are actually very glad that you have drugs available to you – many people don't. You are also glad that you have over a week of quality time between treatments, aren't you? So many people have less than that, why don't you feel pleased that instead of being dead, you have ten good days a month? As for the down days, there are bound to be some new Netflix series coming up. I realise that their email recommendations have so far been way off the mark (*Sex Education*, seriously??), but one of these days they will get it right.

Me: Yes, I suppose so... I could focus on the ten good days rather than the ten bad days.

Pollyanna: That's right. Then, and this is really important, you are extremely glad that you do not seem to be losing your hair – because that would have been really depressing, the rest of your life with bald patches...

Me: Oh yes, that is true, I hadn't thought of that... yes, that is something to be very glad about.

Pollyanna: Finally, you can hope that as you become de-sensitised to the drugs, your good to bad day ratio will improve. That gives you a reason to eat healthily, stop with the chocolate biscuits, and gives you a goal to work towards. You will also get used to scheduling your life with these new parameters, it is not rocket science...

Me: Thank you, Pollyanna, that was a great help. You can go now!

Pollyanna: And bear in mind, that if this drug stops working, the next one – if there is one, will be worse – and you will look back longingly to this time...

Me: You were doing so well until that, and now you have ruined it...

Pollyanna *(shrugging)*: It's true...

In spite of my efforts to think positively, when my fourth cycle of the T-DM1 treatment was due, I turned up at the clinic, sat in my chair and when the nurse asked politely how I was, I started crying again. The clinic nurse is not used to me crying, so called the doctor. "I feel awful the whole time, my brain is in a fug, I ache all over, I cry every time anyone speaks to me, I can't do anything other than lie around feeling miserable and then just when I start to feel better, it is time for another treatment. And all I can hope for is that this goes on and on. It will never get better. This will be my life from now on. What is the point?"

The doctor looked at me and said gently, "Have you ever had Counselling?" I knew that this time I was not going to get away with an "I don't do counselling, I am fine" – I had snot bubbling out of my nose, tears rolling down my cheeks and was sounding like an hysteric. Counselling was going to happen. I tried a "What can counselling do?" just to save face.

"Just talking to someone will help," answered the doctor.

"But I am talking to you."

"Someone professional."

"You are a professional."

"A professional who is trained for this."

"How can training someone help them to stop you feeling awful?"

"Tino," said the doctor to the nurse, "please make an appointment for Ileana with Mary now. And I mean NOW."

She turned back to me and said, "The first session is free anyway and you haven't had a single session since you were diagnosed. I will just tweak the steroids you are getting as some people are really sensitive to them, and that might help."

Tino took me firmly by the elbow and led me over to the reception desk. "We would like an appointment with Mary," he said decisively, patted me encouragingly on the back and left.

Well, I had had a good run, it had to end sometime.

Miraculously, the steroid tweak had immediate effect, tears dried up, energy levels rose, brain cleared, aches faded, my mood lifted, and, best of all, Pollyanna went back to work. "Did you have a good holiday?" I asked her a little sarcastically, "Wonderful, thank you!" She beamed back at me, "Now, if you wouldn't mind getting out of my way, I have lots to do, no offence but it looks as if no one has done a thing around the house since I went away."

If pearls weren't so hard to find I would have told her what I thought of her. No offence my foot.

After a while, as I got used to things and felt a bit better, I nearly forgot all about side effects, and, also I am afraid, the bit about being more like Hélène – gentle, delicate and self-effacing. Sadly, forgetting is one of the few things that I am getting much better at. I spent one morning immediately after treatment, creating terminal confusion via emails for a saintly and very funny editor of a travel magazine with whom we were trying to arrange a press trip. I had to ring her in the end, in tears of laughter to apologise and explain. She knew about my health situation and replied – also in tears of laughter, "I was about to send you an email telling you not to worry as I know you are on shit-loads of drugs, but then I thought HR would probably want to follow that up with both of us... so I am glad you rang, but can you please go and have a nap or something and I will deal with it."

When the day of my appointment with Mary arrived, I was feeling so completely back to my normal self that I nearly cancelled it. My friends all said severely that I should stop being such a baby and just go. Emma and Kate both know what to say. "Just think of it as another type of medical appointment that you can write about, and it is free..." so I went.

Mary kicked off with a "You can talk about anything you like for an hour. It is all entirely confidential, and nothing you say will be shared with anyone else. Unless you say you are thinking of harming yourself or anyone else, in which case I must inform the appropriate people." I was rather taken aback at this, and promised I was not going to harm either myself or anyone else. In fact, it was rather pleasant talking about myself for almost an hour. It made a change from writing about myself. Mary listened carefully and then started to probe, rather like a dentist with a sharp pick, looking for cavities...

"When you say you cried any time anyone asked you about the new treatment, would you say you are overwhelmed at what has happened to you?"

"No, I was just depressed about the treatment, and now we have fixed the steroid dose, I feel better and don't cry anymore."

"When you say you didn't feel like doing anything, is it because you find no pleasure in life and feel as if you are in a dark tunnel?"

"No, it was just that I was too tired and achy to do anything even though I wanted to."

"When you say that all you wanted to do was go to bed, is bed an escape from reality for you?"

"No, I mean I could have lain on a sofa or deckchair as well, I just needed to lie down."

Then I came clean about my book, my slightly mocking riff on Counselling, my psychic housekeeping, my Pollyanna and my theory of sweeping things under the carpet. I expected her to explain why this was terrible and I shouldn't bottle things up like that.

Instead, she gave me a big smile and said, "You don't need counselling, Pollyanna is a terrific hire and is doing an excellent job for you, you seem to live entirely in the present, which is what people spend years trying to achieve."

"I can't say I take much credit for that," I said, "I mean, when you have a really bad memory and no idea how much future you have, you do end up living in the present..."

"Well, that is what Buddhism tries to teach us, and so all I can say is keep doing whatever you are doing. In fact, I would love to read your book, which I will go and buy later today, and perhaps you would talk to some of my weepier ladies, the ones who break down and start crying in the supermarket?" (Oops, an unfortunate typo put "dying in supermarkets," lucky I caught that...) To show how empathetic I was, I told her that I too used to breakdown and cry in supermarkets – *before* I had cancer – especially in the downtown Harrow branch of Tesco's. But then I discovered Waitrose and that doesn't happen anymore, so I would be delighted to chat to anyone she thought might find it helpful.

All in all, I thought, as I swung happily out of the clinic, Counselling was an excellent thing, and I had even sold another copy of my book, so Short Books will be pleased too. Pollyanna will probably want a raise, but a pearl is a pearl.

Gifts

Beware of Greeks bearing gifts is a well-known trope from the Aeneid, but honestly, it is a two-way street; gifts brought to Greeks are not without dangers either... I am not sure why, but people have decided that the perfect little gift to bring me when visiting is tea, and sadly not boxes of 100 Earl Grey and English Breakfast tea bags, which are always useful – no, I have a cupboard bursting with boxes, sachets, pastes, wraps, balls, leaves and flowers. Sencha, Genmaicha, Macha, Ginseng, Hibiscus, berry infusions, Rooibos, turmeric, and worst of all, umpteen tins and chests of antique teas where there is no name in English at all, just mysterious Chinese and Japanese characters. In pride of place, however, are three teas from Lithuania brought by a journalist friend who swears they are good for you; *Salvei Sopradega* produces a poison green liquid, *Helesinine Laguun* a bright blue one that looks like lavatory cleaner while *Uheska Vagina* (yes, that is what it is called), is yellow flowers. Luckily all three taste of nothing worse than water in which one has hand-washed a cashmere sweater – the main difference between the three, (and also between them and cashmere sweater hand-washing water) – being that after the *Uheska Vagina*, you have yellow flowers plastered all over your teeth. *

The other type of gift is often a book; books written by people who have found God through suffering, books written by people who have been through grief, books with meditative poems, books written by people who have decided to dump their husbands – possibly after reading too many poems. I don't understand this either. What is wrong with scented candles? I love my friends and I can't wait for Christmas, but please – no more gifts.

---

* The giver of the tricouleur of teas says slightly huffily that they are from Estonia, not Lithuania, and it is *Uheska Vagine*, not Vagina.

Superwoman

Finally meeting Hélène, Prof E's inspiring introduction, was a bit of an eye-opener; I went to sit with her while she was having treatment, and she turned out to be a young, fine-boned bundle of raw energy with a pixie haircut, wearing jeans and a suede jacket, holding down three young children and a high-powered job in an international bank as a project manager. Nothing gentle or self-effacing about her at all, I was thrilled to see. The only concession she makes to having cancer is that she takes the day off work for her treatment, and the day off after it as well.

"I am in charge of complying wiz all ze possible new Brexit regulations, so interesting! I love ze challenge, my team are super understanding of my situation and I absolutely 'ate sitting around at 'ome."

I just goggled at her. I could hardly project manage the supermarket shop at the time and sitting around at home was my idea of heaven. I asked her to describe how having "our" cancer fits into a proper office job.

"Well, to be 'onest, my boss is *fantastique*, my team are great, when it gets too stressful, I just shout at zem and say, *oh la la*, you are all just making a lot of NOISE, go away and sort it out." What a good line, I thought.

"Ze real problem is HR." she continued, "My boss sees me as a very good organiser and someone who always delivers. HR see me as a potential multi-million-pound lawsuit, zey would much razzer I left... Zey worry zat I am going to claim stress is bad for my cancer, so zey insist zat I have an Occupational Therapist at ze office. 'E wants to talk about cancer all ze time, I just want to get on wiz my work. 'E looks at me very intensely wiz big, sad eyes and says things like 'my wife had cancer so you can tell me how you are feeling.' 'E drives me round ze bend."

I said I couldn't think of anything worse and mentally added the Occupational Therapist as another Cancerland official to be avoided...

"Anyway, I 'ave found a way to keep 'im busy," she added, "I have asked 'im to investigate what 'appens if there is a no-deal Brexit, and I am relocated to France – children's schooling, 'ouse 'unting, will my UK 'ealth insurance pay for treatment abroad, so many worries zat stress me…"

Her face split into a huge grin and I looked at her, lost in complete admiration.

We compared notes and swapped tips on how to manage Prof E and stop him from getting over-worked, and agreed that neither of us wanted to ask what happened once this drug we are on stopped working. It turns out that we are both optimists and are sure that someone will figure something out.

As we were talking about Brexit, we wondered what would happen if we couldn't get our drugs anymore, as the key ingredients come from the Continent. We imagined the clinic hiring a luxury charabanc, transforming it into a mobile treatment suite, and organising daily drug runs over to France or Belgium. There is a sit-com in there somewhere…

Her treatment over, Hélène buttoned up her shirt, bounded out of the chair and set off at full steam with me hurrying to keep up with her. "I am going 'ome for a little rest now", she announced. I didn't believe her for one second.

Guardians on Strike

Anthropologists will have it that women are the guardians, of religion, tradition, spirituality, even ethnicity. When we women forget how to do the rituals, all those things will die. I am acutely aware that as the generation of women before us are gathered into dust, we are the ones expected to know how to arrange funerals, prepare Easter dishes, know the rules of fasting, celebrate the Shabbat, observe Ramadan, mix healing pastes, and all the rest of it. As a mixed-cultural person, I have never had more than a smattering of superficial knowledge about any of my cultural heritages, and have always depended on the kindness of aunts, in-laws and cousins to guide me over these uncertain paths which criss-cross each other, come to dead-ends, or peter out in the long grass more often than not. Easter has always been a double whammy of ritual, with half the family Catholic and half Orthodox, each celebrating Easter in a different way and at a different time, meaning we rarely get it right for either. I fear for my descendants, who will be even worse placed than me to ensure any continuity of religion and ethnicity, or any sense of belonging to a tribe. The two Easters of 2019 arrived like breaking waves, with crests just one week apart. I was feeling washed out from the new treatments anyway, and in a spirit of passive rebellion, decided to celebrate neither. Catholic Easter was reduced to a family lunch that would have happened anyway, with just with a few more flowers than usual, but Orthodox Easter the following week, I simply ignored. Easter is tremendously important to Greeks, it is part of the Greek identity whether you are pious or not; huge amounts of fasting, soaking lentils, cooking, baking, church services, egg dyeing, visiting, preparations, candles, feasting and dancing take place over a whole week, while Greece grinds to a standstill. That year, I told my daughter not to come home from Greece, my sons forgot about it anyway, and my only contribution was thumbs-up emojis in response to the tide of "Christ is risen!" messages that flooded in from Greek friends.

In a mood of peacefully heathen serenity, I read another chapter of one of my books on particle physics and quantum theory for idiots, and felt humbled at the immensity, the beauty and the unfathomability of life, at the same time feeling quite strongly that none of it needed anthropomorphising into a religion for me. It certainly didn't call for two consecutive weeks of religious confusion – the first time round trying to feel sad and pious about the (Catholic) Passion for a week, then on Sunday, joyful about the Resurrection Number One with roast lamb and too much chocolate, then on Catholic Easter Monday, instead of eating lamb leftovers and the rest of the chocolate eggs, plunging into deepest Orthodox fasting for another week while feeling sad about the Passion all over again, then another joyful Resurrection with another roast lamb and Easter eggs. Stuff it, I thought (not the lamb, which remained defiantly unstuffed). This guardian resigns, and the next generation will just have to figure it out for themselves.

Odd Shoes

There are days where one shouldn't get out of bed. A particularly challenging travel schedule for June meant that countless hours had to be spent fitting in important scans to see if the new drugs were working, as well as treatment and an appointment with Prof E who, while I had been commuting between Greece and London, had been commuting between Texas and New Zealand. Logistical problems were only solved by rigorous planning and precise timing.

However, when I arrived back from Greece for step one of the choreographed Harley St dance, I was told that my scan, around which the whole performance had been designed, had been cancelled by mistake. After my going into full hysterics on the phone, the scanning centre discovered that they could in fact, offer me a slot later that day. Much later. From that point on, everything went wrong. I failed to get the scanning people to agree that cancelling a scan on the phone with an unknown temporary secretary whose name they hadn't noted was a ridiculous policy that didn't work. Then we had a barney about which insurance company I was with: Olivia O'Boyd of Allianz Dublin, I know you are not my insurer, but both our lives would be so much easier if you just paid my Harley St bills. Then, on my third trip to the bathroom that day (I had been drinking a lot of water), the loo was disgusting... ladies, I know you have cancer, but it doesn't mean you can't put paper down the loo rather than on the floor, and how do you even *get* a pubic hair in the sink? Are you all contortionists?? So I had to have an argument with the reception about that as well. Then, as I was waiting for my scan, all prepped with my radioactive tracer injection which picks out cancer activity for the scanner in a lurid neon light, a team of ambulance men brought in an elderly gentleman who did look as if he had been dead for a while.

"Sorry, we need your room," they said, as I was unceremoniously bundled out with all my belongings. Normally you are told to lie very still for an hour so that the radioactive dye only picks out cancer activity and not any other, but no one seemed to be bothered.

Finally, almost two hours later I was lying on the scanner bed. "Does it matter that we are doing this scan almost an hour too late and I have been rushing around carrying my things like a homeless person on crack cocaine? Will the dye still work?" I asked.

"Hmm, let's see, yes, it is a bit late, but no need to worry," replied the radiologist, "We will compensate for it."

This was the last straw. This scan was to tell me if my cancer, which had recently reoccurred, was responding to the new treatment or not – Prof E was due to plan my future on this, and they were just going to COMPENSATE ME FOR IT? A bunch of flowers, a box of chocolates and a e-note from Funky Pigeon saying, "There are some suspicious areas on your scan report, but we can't really tell what they are as the dye didn't work properly, please accept this token for £12.50 to cover your travel expenses."

"You cannot be serious!" I shouted, leaping off the scanner bed like John McEnroe in his heyday, "What do you mean, compensate for it? Do you just eyeball it? Pin the tail on the donkey? Blind man's buff? I haven't flown back from Greece, risked cholera from your loos, hung around all day as you cocked-up your appointments, been queue-barged by a corpse, all for a scan that you are going to tweak to make up for the fact that the dye stopped working!" Then I spoiled the effect by bursting into tears.

"No, no," said the radiologist in alarm, "I promise you; I don't want to get too technical about it, but it is a setting on the algorithm of the scanner and the scan will be perfect, please don't get upset."

"Well now we will be delayed even longer because I will need five minutes to stop crying, as you can't scan me while I am shaking all over," I sobbed angrily. Then I saw the radiologist look surreptitiously at the nurse and jerk his head a little, and felt that an offer of Counselling was imminent, so I blew my nose on the hospital gown, dried my eyes, thought ruefully how ridiculous I was being, and we finished the scan in impeccable order.

When I stopped by the clinic to pick up my phone charger which I had forgotten there, Tino looked at me curiously. "I love your shoes, very fashionable!" he said. I looked down. I was wearing one grey shoe and one brown one. Of course, nothing was going to have gone smoothly that day. It was in fact a miracle that we had got anything sorted out at all.

The next morning, back at the clinic for my chemo treatment, Tino took my usual observations to get the drugs authorised. Blood pressure, "Fine, amazingly enough", glucose levels, "Fine," weight, "Fine, you even seem to have put on a kilo or two!" Which in Cancerland is usually meant to be a compliment and a good thing, but of course it isn't. Then, in a more serious voice, "Final test; please show me your shoes." Two matching grey shoes. "Good, we can go ahead with the treatment."

The next appointment was with Prof E to discuss the scan results. Luckily, I don't suffer from "scanxiety" but still, I made sure to wear matching shoes again.

"How are you?" he beamed in an exaggerated way.

"Well, I am rather hoping that you will tell me!" I answered, slightly unnerved by the beam.

"I asked you first," he said, so I told him I was fine, though had my doubts about the scan's accuracy. He brushed aside my tell-tale tattling about the corpse and the dirty loos, and said,

"The scan is very clear and shows that your cancer has gone back to sleep, so that is excellent news, couldn't be better, a really good result!" I could feel a "but" hanging there, so I waited. "But, and this is really fascinating," he paused – fascinating your oncologist is not necessarily a good thing – "You seem to have picked up a fungus in your lungs. I have never come across it before, so I am referring you to my colleague Dr Nirvana (yes, really, that is what I heard). It may not be anything of course, as PET scans pick up everything, and even if you were to scan someone with a cold, it would show up as something interesting."

Fungus. I mean really, this was almost as humiliating as the dermatologist exclaiming over *ze zings* embedded in my feet – now I had mushrooms growing in my lungs. What next? It was like having your children sent home from school with head lice all over again. Chemo is cool, cancer is uber cool, fungus is definitely not.

The Lung Doctor

Dr Nirvana was not really his name, but it sounded like that, so let's continue to call him that as it is *such* a good name for a doctor.

"You are not the first to get his name wrong," sighed the PA.

Dr Nirvana certainly lived up to his new name. He listened carefully to me saying that the main symptom was something funny going on with my voice; that I could no longer shout (which for a combustible Greek is a disaster), and that my voice got all quavery when I raised it, making me sound as if I was about to cry rather than striking fear into the heart of radiologists – and just the fact that I sounded tearful made me burst into tears, more often than not. Then he nodded understandingly, saying, "Not the effect you want at all, I am sure." He didn't think it was cancer, he didn't think it was fungus, what he thought was that we should do nothing for a few months and see where the river of life took us. Ommmm......

As it turns out, a letter from Dr Nirvana the next day informed me that, on further reflection, he was of the opinion that what I had was something called Organising Pneumonia. How very satisfying, I thought, not your usual hysterical, drama-queen, out-of-control pneumonia, but *organising.* Calm, unflustered armies of well-drilled cells, who go about their business with quiet efficiency. Just like me. My satisfaction was momentarily disrupted by Dr H, who rang me to say, in lugubrious tones, that he was sorry to read all the letters that had been blizzarding around the various Harley St clinics I attend. Dr H usually only calls when he thinks I am about to die.

"Why?" I asked panicking, "Why are you sorry, what is wrong with the letters? I thought it was all rather good news – not cancer or fungus, just a well-organised pneumonia?"

"No, no," Dr H. said hastily, "I am sure it is all fine, I just wanted to tell you that I was sorry to hear there were any letters at all." Just to be safe, I called Prof E straight away to confirm that everything was OK.

Of course, I repeat, what one must not do is use google irresponsibly when looking up your latest illness. Google throws back at you the most frequently asked questions, of which the first is always, "Is illness X fatal?" Even if you look up hay-fever or the common cold, this is the question that tops the polls. There is practically no illness that can be confidently categorised as non-fatal – even hiccups can kill, so skip that question and move straight onto the more interesting things. And for the sake of everyone else, please, please refrain from ever typing in morbid questions so that Google takes a deep breath and calms down a bit.

Life in the Fast Lane

Disappointingly, the organising pneumonia turned out to be nothing as satisfying as I had imagined. They are not calm and rational immune cells. Quite the contrary, rather like a phantom pregnancy, the body, totally confused by years of hard-core drugs, is fantasising that its lungs are being attacked by pneumonia bacteria, and sends in the immune cell troops to counterattack. The lungs find this highly irritating, unsurprisingly, and respond with an infection. A two-month course of mega-steroids to dampen down the immune system is the frontline treatment. I resisted this as long as I could as they had made me so weepy during chemo, and mega doses make you blow up like a balloon (yes, I know, totally superficial of me), but after another month things were no better. My friend Afreen, a gentle yet strangely forceful person who has lived with an auto-immune disease for 35 years and has been on steroids for most of them, told me to man up, stop being such a baby and take the medicine. "They will make you feel better straight away," she said firmly. "Yes ma'am," was the only possible answer, so back I went to Dr Nirvana with the good news that I was going to be sensible.

"Excellent! Now, you may experience mood swings, so do warn everyone that if you are cranky or tearful it is not you, it is just the drugs" said Dr Nirvana kindly, "You could become a bit hyper and your digestive system might be a bit off..."

"I might warn them about that too while I am at it," I said considerately.

Hyper doesn't really do justice to the bliss of high-dose steroids. I could never inhale smoke without collapsing into embarrassing choking fits, and I hated being dizzy, giggly and stupid, so was never a pot smoker. I was too much of a control enjoyer (I refuse to call it freak) for hallucinogenic drugs, so as an art student and set painter in New York in the early '80s, coke and speed were my choices. They cleared the head, blew away any fog or fatigue, gave you boundless energy and focus, and they boosted whatever you were normally to the power of ten. During chemo, I would occasionally think a little wistfully about them, but those days are past. Now I was being prescribed the real deal.

The prescription coincided with a ten-day walking holiday in the Alps, with some very athletic alpine friends which I had been dreading for two reasons. Firstly, walking uphill had become a bit of a problem, and Florian had not helped my morale by saying (implausibly) that he would tailor all the walks to my level, adding that if I preferred, I could just sit at home with one of the group who I hadn't seen for 35 years (and even then we had not really been friends), as she had a problem with a dodgy hip replacement and couldn't walk either. Secondly, one of the friends was Florian's best buddy whom I love, but when the two of them get together, Florian regresses to the irritating state in which he was when I first met him, and the correction of which took 30 years of hard work. All in all, I had been feeling rather glum about the whole thing.

Imagine my joy when I discovered that 40mg of prednisolone do exactly the same thing as a line of coke, plus, you can make a clear announcement on day 1 that if you are bad tempered and snap at people, i.e. Florian and his best friend, they must understand that it is the meds. You can also say that you apologise in advance, glaring pointedly at the two of them, and adding that they would be wise not to irritate you. I powered up and down the mountains every day for four hours, felt like a million dollars, and told Florian and his friend to stop mansplaining and expecting to be waited on hand and foot. It was like having a vacation to my 20s. Plus I lost two kilos. Daily life was similarly affected. Some people become listless, but I turned into a whirling dervish, a Duracell bunny, mercilessly and furiously polishing – silver, wood, mirrors, dogs – anything that didn't move out of my way fast enough. I moved furniture, placed candles, plumped cushions, scrubbed pans and floors till midnight most nights, totally unable to sit still. Every cupboard and drawer was ruthlessly audited, contents colour co-ordinated, mending done, prunings given to charity, clothes-hangers all turned to line up in the same direction, socks matched. At one point, I even tackled the office filing cabinet and bank statements; all invoices and receipts are now in apple pie order going back to 1997, and 80 kilos of paper have been chucked. (I mean recycled if the Eco-warrior is reading this.) It was almost scary; like Moira Shearer in *The Red Shoes*, "If someone doesn't stop me," I thought, "I will dance myself to death."

Olympic Gold

Going to the gym on steroids makes it crystal clear why athletes dope. You leap onto the rowing machine and push violently back and forth, while chatting at full volume. You gaily pick up 15 kilo weights in each hand and, to the alarm of the trainer, swing them merrily around your head at top speed till he gets dizzy trying to keep up and stop you knocking yourself or someone else out. Crunches? Pffff… "If you don't tell me when to stop, I will just keep doing these forever." Pull-overs and fly-overs till the cows come home. "Haven't you got anything heavier than this??" Star jumps on the trampoline? "Wheeeeeeeeee!!!!!!"

The trainer finally cracks, removes any dangerous objects from your vicinity and says, "Why don't we do some mindfulness positions on the floor mat?" I had never head of the "Sleeping Baby" pose, but he was strangely adamant we should do it for around ten minutes, which took us to the end of the session.

The next day of course, I woke up unable to move and decided not to go to the gym again till my steroids were reduced, to everyone's relief.

I came in for a lot of teasing, but to be honest, people expect Superwoman feats from me most of the time, and I need a little help. Danae decided that she was moving back to London from Athens for a few months, with countless, vacuum-packed boxes of clobber, just when I had scheduled her bedroom to be redecorated. I looked despairingly at the already full room that had to be emptied for the decorator who was coming the day before she was due back, and wondered where her packing cases were going to go. A sensible start would be chucking out the rubbish that she wouldn't miss – old boxes, a body painting kit for 12-year-olds, books called "The Idiot's Guide to Something or Other" that if she hadn't read by now, would certainly not be of any help. After an hour, I had around four cardboard boxes of junk ready to throw away. As sod's law would have it, the Eco-warrior was around.

"Mummy," he said sternly, "What have we said about throwing away other people's things?"

"But darling it is a 12-year-old's body-painting kit, I am sure Danae won't want it."

"But there is nothing wrong with it, you can't throw it away. I have told you, let me take care of recycling so you don't just chuck things."

"But my angel, there are two boxes of books that have been lying in the hall for almost two years that you promised to get rid of, and they are still there, how can I give you yet more things to deal with?"

"I didn't know I was supposed to do anything with them."

Honestly, Eco-warriors....

"Well, you can put the body-painting kit in your room then," I said to conciliate him, "but I have to make room for Danae's umpteen imminently arriving packing boxes and then empty it all again for the decorators."

"Fine, I will put it all in my room."

His room by now is crammed with tottering piles of junk that he will one day sort out and recycle, but hasn't had the time to do so for about a year and a half, and the tottering piles just keep growing. No wonder he has moved out.

"By the way, Mummy," wrote Danae from Athens, "Don't forget that Cordelia is coming to stay from Hong Kong for a few weeks with several boxes of cold weather stuff she wants to leave with us, so I hope the room will be ready by November 10th, and

70

I am seriously worried about your taste, so while I am very grateful that you are doing my room, please let Auntie Paola check everything before you decide anything."

How is one supposed to cope with all this without steroids?

I was moaning about this one day to Afreen, my friend who is also on steroids, who also has the decorators round at her cottage in Wales. "I had sorted out 12 bags of outdoor jackets and coats to take to the charity shop – *12 black dustbin bags* – and there are only the two of us," she said. "I turned my back for five minutes, and Richard (her husband), had been in there like a family of weasels and taken out at least half. I said, 'But darling, you haven't worn those for at least ten years, and they don't even fit you any more'. He just said, 'Well, they might fit a guest who comes to stay' 'What guest?' I said, 'Who will come and stay until we have hot water and heating, and how are we going to get that done unless I can empty these rooms so the builders can finish?'"

We sighed in sympathy and each of us thoughtfully swallowed an extra 5mg of Prednisolone.

Afreen and I may have been missing a trick, though, on the decorating front. Collapsed in front of the television one evening, I saw an advertisement for Wayfair.com, a website I had become very familiar with as you can browse all sorts of furniture and accessories, which, if not poo-poohed by your daughter, can be delivered to your door. The lady in the advert was dressed to kill, twirling gaily around her house which had been apparently decorated entirely with items delivered by Wayfair.com. She coyly peeped around every door, smiling enticingly, and said to camera, "Oh I love my house, it is so pretty," and then twirled off into the kitchen where her adorable set of nesting Wayfair.com-ordered children were sitting, saying, "Mother, you have such wonderful taste and thank you for redecorating the house so beautifully and efficiently while having cancer and cancer therapy and steroids!" No one was telling her she was being controlling or invasive or domineering. No one was telling her off for being insensitive, no one was lecturing her on empowering other people rather than doing it all herself, and no one was suggesting she lie down and chill. Then the doorbell rang, she twirled off to answer it and there stood a Paul Newman look-alike delivery man from Wayfair.com with yet another piece of furniture. Her face lit up. She clearly knew him, was even expecting him. "Hello!" She breathed dizzily, "Hello to you too", breathed back the delivery man. I would bet my last dollar that they had been having it off on the Wayfair.com sofa for weeks. A *Brief Encounter* for our times. Vistas of thrilling extramarital affairs suddenly opened up in front of me. Wayfair.com, Jim Lawrence, Peter Jones, a slight hitch is that our extremely friendly DHL delivery driver who is the only one who can find our house, is a shy lesbian, but these are minor obstacles. The real problem is to get my daughter to allow me to get on with her room, and the Eco-warrior to empty the porch of discarded telescopes, broken amplifiers and cardboard boxes full of dictionaries, so that my Paul Newman could actually get to the doorbell. I am missing out on so much.

Hospital Stays

My position has always been to avoid these whenever possible, the main reason being that you abdicate all control over your life – and they take away your sleeping pills. At 9.30 in the evening the nurse will ask if you would like *one of your own* sleeping pills, but you have to swallow it now in front of her. How do I know at 9.30 if I will need one or not? What I want is to keep my pills with me, like a talisman, and then if I feel like taking one at midnight, I will. But no, instead you are dosed up on antibiotics as soon as you check in, and have little say over what comes next. So for all these reasons, when I woke up one morning with a temperature of 38 – which is the danger point for people on chemo and you are supposed to rush to hospital in case you turn septic all over – I hesitated. This sepsis is called being Neutropenic, in case you are hoping for serious information from this book. In the end, and very reluctantly, I did call the hospital as deep down I am an obedient and rule-respecting person. "I am feeling fine, though, and as long as you are happy for me to stay home and take paracetamol, that would be great," I said. No, as it turns out, they were not at all happy for me to stay home and take paracetamol. In fact, the only thing that would make them happy would be if I presented myself at the hospital entrance for admission within two hours. I grumpily packed an overnight bag, carefully hid my sleeping pills in a side pocket, and checked in.

"We need a urine sample," said the young Eastern European nurse who came to take my vitals. "Please can you pee into a sock?"

I gawped at her. This was a first for me. I have peed into many things but never a sock.

"Are you sure?" I asked cautiously.

"Yes, I am sure."

"You don't want to quickly check that again?"

"Please, just take this sock and pee into it."

She then held out a jug.

"Oh," I said in relief, "You mean a jug!"

"Yes," she replied a little impatiently, "Is what I said, a sock."

I gave up and meekly peed into the sock-jug for her. Sock, jug, potato potahto...

If she says something needs amputating though, I might get her to use google translate first.

That was the highlight, though. I didn't like the doctor who came in to explain why I was there – she just spouted protocol and policy at me – then I kicked up a fuss about not wanting to take antibiotics till they had proven that there was a bacterial infection. I also insisted that I didn't want to spend the night, so in the end, they threw their hands in the air and discharged me. On the way home, I bragged triumphantly to my silently driving husband that I was in total control, the doctors were all jobs-worthies, that I knew my body better than them, and that what my body was telling me was that it was perfectly alright and didn't need antibiotics or monitoring. Patient Empowerment is what it is all about. I patted my thigh complacently and said, rather as to a dog, "Good body."

The next morning, I woke up with a fever of 40 degrees, and my husband wordlessly drove me back to the hospital. I had to apologise to everyone for having made such a fuss the day before, and promised that I would do everything they said. My consultant dropped round to make sure that I wasn't planning to escape, and I stayed for three days, enjoyed lying in bed, ordering from room service, getting a few visitors, watching *Law and Order* and, crucially, having a break from the frenetic steroid-fuelled housekeeping that was exhausting me, but that I couldn't stop doing. And they didn't take my sleeping pills away from me. As it turned out, there was nothing wrong with me, just a virus, and I could have stayed home, so I could still tell my husband that I did know my body better than the doctors. "Good body."

He said nothing, and then I understood that actually, staying in hospital is primarily to stop your family worrying, as they do not trust that you know your body as well as you think you do. All in all, best to do what you are told the first time round.

So, with this in mind, the next time I picked up what I knew beyond a shadow of doubt to be a virus caught from the Lawyer son, when my fever spiked at 38, I turned up at the hospital with no argument and with my overnight bag packed.

Something was going on though… the ward was discreetly panicking with small groups of people huddled in corners, and a gaggle of hostile-looking medics in scrubs glaring around them. A nurse hissed at me, "Sorry, we are dealing with an Incident, you will have to wait a bit."

Eventually, I was settled in and all was as expected, until at midnight, a night nurse appeared wearing full protective mask, hairnet, gloves and plastic apron.

"What is going on?" I asked, "Why are you wearing all that gear?"

"It is standard practice," he replied primly.

"No it isn't," I said sternly, "I am in and out of here almost as much as you are, and I have never seen this before."

"No, no, perfectly normal, nothing to worry about." He repeated, looking distinctly furtive.

Something clicked in my brain; it was January 2020 and the beginning of the Coronavirus pandemic.

"Oh my God, you have got Coronavirus on the ward, that is it, isn't it? That is what the incident was earlier! Please take this drip out right now so I can leave!"

He sighed, "No, honestly, the reason we are wearing this is entirely because of *you*, until your Covid test results come back, we have to wear this kit. It takes ages to put on and take off, it is a real bore, so please, just pipe down and stay in your room."

On my return home the next day, I could triumphantly reassure all my sneezing and coughing family that we had all tested negatively for Coronavirus, and that I had nearly shut down an entire ward all on my own. It very much reminded me of the old Jewish Joke about the solemn, and expensive occasion of the annual visit of the city doctor to the Shtetl in Poland... Moritz sets off for the village, carefully bearing the urine sample requested by the city doctor for his check-up. In the evening, he comes home, announcing triumphantly to his family of nine children, wife, mother, sister, uncle, nieces, nephews and possibly a few chickens as well, "Good news, we are all healthy!"

***

Accident and Emergency wards in hospitals are not Britain's proudest products. Overworked, overcrowded and undersupplied, any visit there strikes fear into the heart of the sturdiest. The treatment is excellent, but, oh, the hours of waiting, and the waiting rooms...

People living with cancer have one big advantage here, as what with our depressed immune systems and everything else, we get put at the front of the queue, just behind frothing-at-the-mouth overdoses, howling babies, workmen clutching bleeding heads, and well ahead of swollen-ankled diabetics and people on crutches. And this was even truer during the time of Covid.

My elderly, Viennese neighbour for whom I occasionally did shopping, wanted to make me an apple strudel as a thank-you, so I dug out a mandolin slicer and brought it over to her house along with a bag of fat raisins and some apples.

"Oh my," said her carer who opened the door. "I nearly cut my finger off with one of those, I won't use them." The apple strudel was delicious, and was eaten in one morning (mainly by me). So, in a moment of Lockdown culinary ambition, I decided to make one myself. I had raisins, apples and a mandolin after all, what could go wrong? The apple slid like silk through the mandolin blade, leaving perfect round disks of translucent apple slices, then there was a slight rasp, and I realised that my finger had also slid like silk through the mandolin, just as the neighbour's carer had warned. I shoved my finger in my mouth, sucking hard to stop the bleeding, fled to the bathroom cabinet and with my eyes almost closed, managed to wrap a roll of gauze and tape over the finger, and called my husband to drive me to the A and E. I am always cool in a crisis, so while he looked for the car keys, I went to find my fingertip to bring it to the hospital with me in case they could sew it back on. The pile of sliced apples glinted enticingly, so I started to eat them partly to see if the fingertip was there, partly because I am greedy. Halfway through the heap of slices, I found a small, perfect, translucent disk of what could either have been sliced apple core or sliced fingertip. It tasted of nothing so I ate it anyway, then continued to the end of the heap of sliced apples. No fingertip to be seen so I guessed it was the bit I had eaten. When I told the nurse at the hospital that I had probably eaten the fingertip, she said consolingly not to worry, you can't sew them back on anyway. Mandolins are, it turns out, well known causes of injury, "finger food" has a whole new meaning, and I am the cool new auntie for the children of a friend of mine who all wanted to know exactly what the finger tasted of. "Apple," was all I could say.

Crying over Spilt Milk

One shouldn't, but I did. All my life, I have been good with my hands. I have painted, drawn, played the piano, sewn, cooked, glued, carpentered, welded and sculpted. I am not a perfectionist, but I have always been fast and capable. Progressively though, with my T-DM1 treatment, I see that I am changing. My sister is clumsy and breaks things. My son cannot be trusted to carry a glass of water or a tray. I tut-tut in an irritated way and clear up, quickly and efficiently, after them. Now though, I am the one spilling, dropping and breaking. Saucepans take one look at me and tip themselves over, glasses topple in front of me like dominoes. Stools get fallen over, vases get smashed – it is non-stop. The week after I had sliced off the tip of my finger, I had a nosebleed, rushed to the bathroom, and in whipping off my shirt to soak it before it stained, sprayed blood over two bathmats, and sent a little stone Roman bowl flying to the ground where it smashed. In the evening, I broke three glasses and chipped two bowls. The next day, I burned my hand ironing, fell over a footstool and cut my leg. "Slow down!" said my husband, "I can't keep taking you to the hospital every other day."

The day after that I spilt hot broth onto my stomach while stirring the stockpot and had to spend the afternoon with a bag of frozen peas clamped to my waistband. In the evening, I tipped over what remained of the hot broth, and in trying to catch it, knocked over a bowl of lentils which followed the stream of soup onto the kitchen floor. The bowl cracked, followed by me. I sat down and burst into tears. It wasn't the spills or the cuts and burns, it was that I was turning into someone else. For the first time, I felt that the cancer was taking me over, like an evil demon possessing me. Until then, I had always been myself; me with hair, me without hair, me with achy legs, me with a bad memory, me wanting to have a nap, me being cranky, me with lopsided boobs, me with a rash… but me with clumsy hands? No, that was not me. My hands were no longer the hands that I had loved for so many years – they were someone else's; my sister's perhaps, or even my son's.

My cousin Maria, who knows all my buttons, said to me in an encouraging voice,

"Just imagine you are a very important and highly skilled intensive care nurse."

Yes, I thought with a glow of satisfaction, I can imagine that.

"Now," she continued, "Are you rushing around dropping things, tripping over patients and ripping out wires by mistake, or are you doing everything slowly and carefully?"

"Slowly and carefully," agreed the newly promoted IC nurse.

"Right," said Maria, "Now, imagine the kitchen is your theatre of operations, your ER."

"OK," I said, "and perhaps George Clooney could be there too doing the drying up?"

"Yes, whatever," said Maria.

"Don't worry, Mummy," said Danae, "It is Mercury in retrograde. But seriously, you just need to slow down and practise mindfulness."

Now, on top of all the other things I have to put up with, I have to buy two sets of scrubs to wear in the kitchen and become *mindful*, just when I am getting the hang of becoming gleefully *mindless*. I can't catch a break.

Fantastical Beasts

The follow-up appointment with Dr Nirvana was great. I heard with pleasure that my organising pneumonia was quite likely to return; it is a rare condition, but one that can be expected with my drug regime of T-DM1s. If it did, it would mean a longer if slightly lower course of steroids. "I hope you don't mind them too much," said Dr N naively.

I had to make an effort not to grin like a Cheshire cat, as it is never wise to let your doctors know just how much you enjoy their drugs, but I am an honest person.

"Mind them? Are you serious? I am in heaven! That's why I am so pleased with the misnomer I have now attached to you – Dr Nirvana, bliss pills on tap."

I then described my state of heightened activity, the perfect order reigning in my filing cabinets, the beeswax sheen gleaming from every surface at home, the baroque flower arrangements, weeded flowerpots and polished silver.

"Hmm," said Dr N. "Perhaps I ought to prescribe some for myself." He subsided into a thoughtful silence before shaking himself out of it.

"Anyway, I will keep a close eye on you from now on. Do you need more pills? I can now send prescriptions remotely. It is amazing."

I looked at him nonplussed, "Do you mean that you have email?"

"Yes, and there is this astonishing thing called the world wide web that is also really useful. Stacey is my virtual secretary; she doesn't even need to set foot in my rooms here."

Dr Nirvana is young and brilliant and grew up in the digital world, so I hoped that he was being ironic rather than showing worrying signs of eccentricity.

As he is obviously destined to be another highly skilled technician in my pit-stop with whom I am hopefully going to have a long and successful professional relationship, I felt that I was honour-bound to tell him that I was writing volume two of my medical memoirs, and that anything he said was liable to be written down and twisted out of shape for comic or dramatic effect, but that I would fly it by him before it got published. I pushed a specially signed copy of volume one across his desk to him and he grinned happily.

"Splendid! Is Prof E in it?"

"Of course, he makes an early entrance!"

"And Mr G?"

"Naturally!"

"Great, can't wait to read it!"

The idea that Stacey might be a figment of Dr Nirvana's imagination and that his comments about email and the internet might not have been meant ironically, was of some concern. Dimly, in a corner of my mind, I was reminded of an encounter with a very strange yet weirdly charismatic client a few years ago.

Nicholas D, with 20 million euros to spend on an estate on the island of Ithaca, entered my life through a real estate pal of mine. It had to be Ithaca, as Nicholas was a Yorkshire-bred Greek living in exile and yearning to return to his spiritual home. Nicholas appeared nowhere on google searches, the four-page letter he wrote to me about himself, ("I am sure you will want to be reassured that I am a bona fide buyer,") mentioned that having sold his AI (Artificial Intelligence for those who don't keep up) company for squillions, he had paid a huge sum of money to be erased from Google's entire data bank. So far, so plausible.

Nicholas started writing to me – wisps of poems, shreds of philosophy, tales of his life, sepia coloured prints of him serving out his Greek military service on the Bulgarian frontier, the name of his dog, his obsession with Ithaca and Odysseus, moody photos from the Pennines, the thrill of exploring the frontiers of AI, the trauma of his divorce from his UK wife, the damage that had caused to his whole psychological state ("I have very weak nerves now, one of the reasons I want to retire to a quiet Greek Island with my dogs"), and how he couldn't sleep at night thinking about the beauty of the Ithaca estate I had shown him. We arranged to meet in Ithaca where I happened to be.

"I will drive my new Tesla from Italy down to Greece and then cross over by ferry with it to Ithaca," he said, "I will be there in five days max."

Well, reports came every day from Nicholas… the Albanian border had closed and he had had to re-route through Serbia. There were no Tesla charging points in Serbia. He was lost as the sat nav didn't work. He was sleeping in a forest in the car as it had run out of battery. He was waiting for an old friend to drive up and rescue him as he was cold and tired and his two dogs were howling, plus he thought he had seen a bear. He was on his way to Thessaloniki, he had finally got to Greece, glory be to God, he had now, however, fallen ill with badly shaken nerves. He was going to need two days to settle the dogs and recover. He could meet me in Athens, he could still make it to Ithaca but a week later. He couldn't make it to Ithaca after all.

We agreed to meet in London two weeks later, but this time, I asked the real estate pal to get a letter of comfort from Nicholas' bank. The next day we received screen shots of six different bank accounts holding 20 million euros cash – with a somewhat strange choice of provider (no offence, Bank of Piraeus), but well-stocked nonetheless.

The day of his arrival in London dawned, but no Nicholas. Being in London had brought back the trauma of his divorce and losing his home. Being in London was not good for his nerves, he was back in bed with a fever. Being in London was impossible so he had taken a private plane to the South of France. Then, he was feeling better, he was so sorry, he was going to stay in Antibes for two days unpacking some new equipment for his Wally Yacht, (photos attached of him unpacking crates of equipment with a happy smile). He was going to go skiing for two days and then fly on a private plane from Lyon to Kidderminster airport. Oh dear, the Route N26 from Val D'Isère to Lyon airport was closed by a massive avalanche, the plane had left without him, he wasn't going to be able to make it. At this point, fascinating as his stories had been, both the real estate pal and myself felt that this had possibly strayed over into crazy territory. We started googling. It turned out that yes, there had been a plane flying an empty leg from Lyon to Kidderminster, and yes, Route N26 had been closed by a huge avalanche. It was perplexingly obvious that both explanations we were facing were equally implausible; that his stories were all true, or that he had been inventing the whole thing with a huge amount of research. Friends were taking bets as to which was the least likely. Emma said it was obvious he was a phony, as did Florian.

"What kind of idiot drives a Tesla through the Balkans?" said my Greek cousin, missing the point completely. On the other side was Emma's husband Andrew, who is a barrister and a circuit judge who has spent his whole career poking holes in testimonies and sniffing out fabrication.

"I say genuine – no one would go to that trouble just for fun," he said.

"I'll tell you what," said the real estate pal, "Let me call in a favour from someone at the Bank of Piraeus."

The next day he rang me. "The screen shots of the bank accounts have been photo-shopped. Perfectly done – but the background colour was from two years ago."

We wrote to Nicholas as kindly as we could to tell him the game was up, but we would be delighted to meet him anyway and get to know the real Nicholas. Probably in a bed-sit in Darlington.

The last I heard from Nicholas was a few months later when he texted me (obviously by mistake, thinking I was someone else), saying "Come down to the yacht at Antibes Harbour for supper at eight tonight, I have just done the shopping and will cook us something delicious."

"Hi Nicholas," I replied enthusiastically, "It's Ileana here, so nice to hear from you, dinner sounds great but perhaps Yorkshire might be more realistic?"

Nicholas was a good sport and wrote back, "Yes, but not nearly so much fun…"

I wonder if the girl ever got her dinner or spent the evening wandering around Antibes looking for a Wally yacht.

The point of this rather long digression is that I then started researching fantasists. Unlike schizophrenics who think that they are Napoleon or God, or confabulists who cannot remember who they are so try to fill in the gaps as best they can, a fantasist knows perfectly well that he is not Napoleon or God, he is just profoundly dissatisfied with his life, and prefers to pretend. And guess what the number one identity of choice is for a fantasist? Yes, *a doctor*. There have been documented cases of fantasists hiring rooms in Harley St, wandering around hospitals in scrubs carrying stethoscopes, and who *have even been known to try to conduct surgeries.* That is when Dr Nirvana's remark about his virtual secretary rang a faint echo of an alarm bell deep in the limbic part of my brain.

Dr Nirvana is of course totally kosher, Stacey exists most beautifully and efficiently, and his excitement about remote prescriptions referred to a high-tech secure portal, and not to a belated discovery of the internet in general.

The Cancer Sistas

"Hi all," I read in an email from a small, informal, travel discussion group to which I belong,

"Following my last email suggesting we club together to buy John a present for his forthcoming prostate operation, I can now update you." I had suggested a nice bunch of flowers as something appropriate and pleasant to receive, hinting that I had liked that when I was in hospital...

"John had his surgery last week for his prostate, and is at home recovering.

Kind Jenny, the GM of Highclass Hall, has offered us a great deal for two nights which, having sounded out both John's wife and his business partner, both say is just the ticket.

I've agreed two nights for £700 in total with a confirmed massive upgrade.

So far, the following friends have agreed to chip in:
Me x £100
Tom x £100
Dick x £100
Harry x £100
Please do let me know if anyone else wants to contribute and I can arrange accordingly. It absolutely doesn't need to be £100."

Oh, so no pressure then... no one will mind appearing as "Ileana x £10" after that.

I replied: "Thank you so much but I am sending John something privately, which, as I have had cancer for over three years and have never got so much as a card from anyone of you, including John, is jolly nice of me I feel!"

Bursting with indignation I showed this highly offensive missive to my sister and husband.

"Very silly of you to write back," said Florian disapprovingly, "You should just ignore things like that and not reply."

"I told you to always check with me first before sending cross emails," said my sister equally disapprovingly.

So I sent an apology, pointedly playing the cancer card by blaming my irritability on recent chemo (true), to which, adding to my fury, I received not a word of reply.

Sometimes, the cancer sistas are the only ones who understand. My friend Lucy got it immediately, "Highclass Hall looks jolly nice, perhaps we can get the group to send us there too?"

Another sista wrote with a rather novel take; "John would be utterly mortified to hear friends were handing round a cap on his behalf!" As John is a self-avowedly stingy Scot this was unlikely to be the case, but anyway.

"What I don't understand," said Florian afterwards, "is how you can be so calm and unemotional about the big things like having cancer, and yet get so upset about truly idiotic little things."

I thought about it carefully.

"I think that it is because cancer is completely impersonal. That is the beauty of it. It is totally non-judgemental, doesn't upset you or flatter you, it is neither fair nor unfair, it is just cells growing in a wonky way. It is not some external agent doing something to you. It is part of you. The truly idiotic little things as you call them, are other people being mean/thoughtless/disrespectful/hurtful/unfair/greedy/irritating, whatever, and that is why I get emotional. I find cancer cells much easier to deal with than people sometimes…"

Not a great admission for someone in the service industry, I do realise that.

I am still waiting for a card or flowers from John and Co., in case you are wondering.

Where There is a Will There is a Way

Not wishing my pneumonia to be the only organisers around, I thought it was probably time to update my will. My lawyer of 30 years is by now an old friend, and I don't begrudge the fees as it means the firm can afford the most fabulous offices with panoramic views over the sun-gilded barges of the Thames and across the London skyline. Worth every penny. Plus, they give you free coffee and biscuits, and expect clients to steal the umbrellas, pens, pads and water bottles.

It is not only highly likely that I will pre-decease Florian, but it is also a clear tax advantage to my children if I do so. "See?" I said to Florian, "There is no point trying to die before me, and if I see you trying to, I will just stop taking my pills."

Florian glared at me, "But I don't want to be left alone to deal with things." "Too bad," I said pitilessly, "Neither do I, and I am well on the way to winning this battle. You are fit and healthy, though horribly lazy; you will live a long time, please God, with nothing worse than a bad back as you won't do your exercises and your idea of a workout is watching me on the rowing machine while lying on the mat with three dogs licking your face."

"Now, now, children," said the lawyer, "No fighting, this is not a competition..."

"Yes it is," Florian and I both answered together, "It is a fight to the death – quite literally." We went eyeball to eyeball and understood each other perfectly. There is no way in hell that I am going to be the one left to deal with family admin on my own, and that is that.

Walking home, I asked my husband which of my sisters he would prefer to have moving in with him to look after him and run the house. Marina, my older one, would do anything for anybody and is the soul of selflessness and goodness but is a little bossy and an overly energetic housekeeper, and to be honest, somewhat suggestion resistant. Paola, my younger one, has not got a bossy bone in her body and is a ray of sunshine, but comes with four fat cats, various reptiles, hundreds of lampshades, trimmings, glue and tools, and finds it hilarious when she drops toothpaste on the carpet – and the thought of clearing said toothpaste up would never occur to her.

He thought for a while and then said a little plaintively,

"Do I have to have either of them? Why can't I move back to Germany?"

"Of course, my darling," I assured him, "You can do whatever you like..."

Seriously, I have no intention of leaving my peaceful star-dust eternity in order to control things post-mortem. See, I am not a control freak at all.

The Salt of Life

So, as I learned on my next visit to Prof E, Dr Nirvana and steroids are going to be an intermittent part of my life from now on, along with Prof E's chemo-cocktails. This is fine by me as I love Dr Nirvana and, as I may have mentioned, I also love steroids. I did notice, though, with a certain admiration, how I was managed by Prof E. He had started off by saying "Interesting" about my lung scans, then followed by, "Possibly fungus, nothing to worry about but a little tricky to get rid of." Then "Organising pneumonia, which steroids will clear up", then "This will probably be a chronic condition but I am very relieved as fungus is bad to get," so you leave his rooms feeling extremely pleased that all you have is a chronic inflammatory lung condition along with cancer, a battered liver and a wheezy heart.

"Golly," says Pollyanna to you on your way home, "How lucky can we get!"

In order not to blow up like a balloon when on massive doses of steroids, you have to give up salt. My least favourite Shakespeare play is *King Lear*. I have always been repulsed by mad old men, all the more so after my own father got Alzheimer's and his white-bearded rantings turned him into a sort of demented Old Testament prophet. I used to hide and leave him to my sisters to deal with. Not proud of myself, but in my defence, I was pregnant for most of the time it seemed. This is not a digression, but very much to the point, which is all about salt. The story of Lear is based on a fairy tale that was apparently told from India to the Appalachians, about a foolish old king who one day decided to test his daughters to see which of the three loved him most. The two elder daughters both came up with the requisite amount of loving hyperbole. The youngest simply said that she loved her father as much as meat loved salt. Enraged at her heartlessness, he banished her from the kingdom, but luckily a handsome prince came along, the father was served a salt-free banquet and realised that salt was worth more than any cheap hyperbole. A happy ending was had by everyone, though the king possibly developed a cholesterol problem after that – unless of course he stuck to one tenth of a teaspoon of pink Himalayan salt per day – the story does not tell us.

This is beyond a shadow of doubt the most annoying fairy tale that exists. I can't think what lapse of judgement persuaded Shakespeare to adapt it, and what is more, to make Cordelia even more soppy and irritating than the original princess. First of all, the king sounds like an 18-carat pillock who doesn't deserve any love at all. Second of all, I too would be mad as hell if any child of mine came up with nothing better than "I love you as much as salt," or even worse as Shakespeare has Cordelia say, "I love you as much as duty obliges me to." I mean, seriously, Cordelia love, could you *be* any more self-righteous? The man is your father for heaven's sake, yes, he is a monumental bore, old and disgusting and should not be tottering about heaths in the middle of the night, but just heave your heart into your mouth as you put it, and stop taking yourself so bloody seriously. Teenagers – they never change. Po-faced, entitled, humourless and fanatical. What does it cost to say, "I love you very much Daddy"?

The salt myth surely skipped over Greece on its way from India – no Greek daughter would be so cruel to her father. I will never forget catching a Greek-American girlfriend of mine dangling my one-year-old daughter on her lap and cooing

86

lovingly, "Now, listen to your Auntie Athena and repeat after me, 'Daddy, buy me gold, Daddy buy me gold, yes, that's it, good girl, Daddy, buy me gold.'" Greek daughters are taught wisely from an early age; a win-win situation.

I suppose it is entirely possible that salt was more highly prized in the days before refrigeration, when salt-free meant dysentery, but I have to say that after four days without salt, I didn't miss it one jot. Herbs do the job beautifully, and in fact it wasn't long before I could hardly make myself swallow anything salty as it tasted so disgusting. Plus, one can allow oneself sugar as a reward for being so good. So much for the salt/love equivalency. Salt, vain old men, priggish teenagers, dull Prince Charmings – not for me. Give me chocolate, *Coriolanus*, and fennel seeds any day.

Alas, all good things have to come to an end. After two salt-free months, I had a follow-up appointment with Dr Nirvana to see if the treatment had worked.

"How are you feeling?" he asked.

"Terrific, "I enthused, "I am full of the joys of life and feel ten yours younger, can we perhaps go on with the steroids a little longer?"

"No," he said frowning, "Not a good idea… long-term use has all sorts of undesirable side effects, so we only use them when we have to. In fact, I think we will stop them now, and we will just keep an eye on you. If the pneumonia flares up again, then we can go back to them. But let's hope it doesn't."

I didn't say anything.

You can't win – if you grumble about your drugs your doctor is unhappy, but nothing compared to his unhappiness if he thinks you are developing an unhealthy attachment to them. In his letter he sent to Prof E, he started with the usual "I was pleased to see this lovely lady again, please note that she feels very well and happy on steroids", which is consultant code for "Please do NOT prescribe them anymore as I think she may be seriously addicted".

Mental Flexibility

I was discussing relationships with my daughter who was, at that time, deeply troubled by the negative impact that pity can have on how the world perceives you; how it so often turns you into a victim. I pointed out that whether or not someone pities you largely depends on how you present yourself. Of course, if you are sad or hurting, it is normal for people to feel pity, and it even has an evolutionary benefit amongst some groups of animals – the hurt one will get fed and be looked after till it can fend for itself again. Once you have had enough of being fed and pitied though, you have to show that you can manage on your own, be a contributing member of the group and even look after others. She nodded thoughtfully and said, "Yes, I see that. I mean, no one pities you." I took that as a huge sign of success on my part, even if I do end up doing all the shopping, tidying, floor mopping, cooking and washing up on my own.

A day later, one of the health bulletins that I once subscribed to and from which I now can't seem to unsubscribe, sent me a report from a psychologist about living with a chronic illness and how one must be mentally flexible in order to embrace one's thoughts, and reshape them. One should label them as either helpful (i.e. keep), or not helpful (i.e. banish). I read it with mild interest, with a view to sending it to a friend with depressive tendencies, and only realised afterwards that *I* was the target reader, not someone else. That is how mentally flexible I have become; I had completely forgotten that I was the one with a chronic illness, which is I suppose the ultimate goal and a triumph of mental reshaping.

The idea is essentially that the brain is flexible or plastic and that we can reshape its way of thinking. The word plastic comes from the Greek "*plastis*" which means "a mould," but is also used in Greek when referring to scabby goods and forged money – as in the case of the 200 euro note I recently tried to use in Athens, which was immediately deemed "*plastos*," by the cashier and firmly shoved back at me. So *plastos* money is bad, but a *plastos* brain is good and, according to this health bulletin, is in fact the main tool needed to combat depression. The distinction between "genuine" and "artificial" is deemed irrelevant in psychology –

instead, the new frame of reference is "helpful" or "unhelpful". One day the European Central Bank might come round to this enlightened way of thinking too. "Is it helpful or unhelpful for this bank note to be accepted?" A mentally flexible ECB banker will ask. Helpful clearly, with great potential in the fight against depression. Perhaps it won't surprise you to know that I failed my economics class at university....

I laundered my *plastos* 200-euro bank note at a supermarket famous for selling scabby fruit and vegetables that are two minutes from rotting (i.e. also *plastos*), so economic justice did prevail in the end.

A p.s. on the subject of eating fruit and vegetables in Greece. I cherish my conversations with Maria, a taxi driver I use in Athens. She is the salt of the earth in the best possible sense, and her philosophical ruminations on everything from traffic jams to the human condition always contain gems.

"Fasting in good for you," she pronounced to me recently, "For Lent, I fasted for five whole days, I ate absolutely nothing."

"Nothing at all? For five days?" I repeated incredulously, "Wasn't that a bit extreme? You must have eaten something."

"No," she replied firmly. "Absolutely nothing."

"What, not even lentils? Even the priests eat lentils." (The usual Greek Lenten fasting staple.)

"Well yes, I mean of course I ate lentils."

"And potatoes?"

"Yes, some potatoes."

"What about pasta?"

"Yes, of course, some pasta, but just with tomatoes."

"Anything else?"

"Not really, just bread, rice, vegetables, fruit, you know, that sort of thing, but no animal products and no olive oil, so no, nothing at all."

To a Greek, veganism is the equivalent of not eating.

***

Speaking of diets, cancer patients are often bombarded with information about what to eat and what not to, so when my friend Paula was recently diagnosed with lung cancer, I went to visit her in hospital to pass on helpful tips such as what juicing machine to buy, how to make kale palatable (oven baked strips), broccoli recipes, plus other useful techniques such as how to get information out of doctors (should one want to). My final gift was to pass on my stash of Missoni turbans (oops, spell check wanted to write Missoni *turnips* – designer vegetables anyone?), with a, "Don't throw them away in case I ever need them back again."

She asked me if, like her cancerous friend, Louise, my cheerfulness was due to my taking "happy pills". I have often wondered what I would answer if someone asked me how I could be happy when faced with relatively imminent mortality. Paula's question raised this again. Yes, we all know that life comes to an end, so as long as you are leaving behind your loved ones and friends in reasonable working order, why should that knowledge stop us enjoying life in the meantime? But apparently it does. It is what differentiates us from animals, it is the curse of the fruit of the tree of knowledge, Eve's terrible gift to humanity. In the end, the best I could come up with was that no matter how pleasant anything is, how relaxing the beach, how beautiful the scenery, how lovely the music, happiness is only a moment; the brain is restless, so if it goes on for longer, it gets boring and I can only experience it for so long before wanting to do something else. In other words, the secret of enjoying life is to have a very short attention span.

Mother-Daughter Talks

There are some seminal moments in all mothers' lives when they have to have a talk with their daughters. The first one is about not getting into cars with strange men offering sweeties, or not looking at photos proffered by single men wearing raincoats. Mind you, my six-year-old daughter and her little friend Anja were walking home from kindergarten one day (children in Germany walk to and from school, with brightly coloured satchels on their backs), when they were stopped by a man who did exactly that – asking them if they wanted to see his photos.

Anja said no, but my daughter, whose interest in photography has remained a constant in her life, looked at what he was showing them. "Hmph," she said in that dismissive way that six-year-olds have, "My daddy's is MUCH bigger than that," and the two little girls walked on without a backward glance. The man, literally crestfallen, was never seen in our neighbourhood again.

When daughters get a little older, there is the talk about what to expect every month, followed by the awkward "How to avoid getting pregnant or an STD" talk. This is the one where the daughter inevitably knows much more than you do, has been hoping she has been spared from it, and if not thus spared, is accompanied by huge amounts of eye-rolling, grimacing and hair tossing. This is shortly followed by the "Why you cannot go out looking like that" talk, and then the "Why you have to be nice to Mummy when she is having hot flashes" talk. Some talks are less universal, such as "Why Daddy is leaving with a 25-year-old blonde", or "Why Mummy is taking you all to live with a new Daddy and some bratty younger children", but basically, you could be forgiven for thinking that that is about it as far as talks go.

No such luck, it appears. There is one final one. I was discussing, as one does, with some girlfriends, the topic of exit strategies. We did seem to agree that the most important of all the human rights is the right to choose how and when to end your life. Having agreed on this, Camilla, who is a tall, beautiful Swedish girl with fearless blue eyes and a Valkyrie look about her, told us about the Mother-Daughter talk she was having with her 80-year-old mother in Stockholm. The mother was still living with Camilla's father in a large old house in the Swedish countryside, and was resistant to learning about emails and using a computer.

"Ma-ma," Camilla said to her, in her lilting Swedish accent, "Ma-ma, it is so impractical for you to live in such isolation without internet or emails. You are getting older, you are nearing the end of your life, you are going to have to learn about all this. If not, you will have to downsize and move to a smaller house in town, otherwise, when it is time for you to arrange for pills to help you die with dignity, how will you find the right doctor or nurse to help you? You have to be responsible and think about these things."

"*Nej, Nej,*" said Ma-ma in alarm, "*Nej,* Camilla, I don't want to learn to use a computer or downsize or move to town or arrange for pills to help me die."

"But Ma-ma, be reasonable, you will have to, it is no good sticking your head in the sand and pretending it will all be fine."

"*Nej,* Camilla," said Ma-ma again. "Please stop this, I am not going to downsize, and I am not going to order pills over the internet."

"You see?" said Camilla turning to us for sympathy, "What can I do?"

An interesting sidenote; I looked up, "How to say no in Swedish" (as I am nothing if not thorough about fact-checking), and Google threw up seven websites about Chlamydia and other STDs, so perhaps in Sweden, at least one of those mother-daughter talks seems to have fallen by the wayside and needs restoring, with some thought given on how to make its message clearer, or at least, how to say *"Nej"*.

Another friend said that her daughters spent their whole time arguing about who was getting what after she died, while she would point out, to no effect at all, that she was still alive and not about to die as far as she knew. My problem is the opposite. I am trying to arrange everything for after I am gone, and my family all stick their fingers in their ears and go "Lalalalala" and "You are going to live another 30 years", which I clearly am not going to do. "*Nej,*" I feel like saying, "*Nej,* and will someone please now help Ma-ma google exit strategies?"

We did all agree though that giving obscene amounts of money to the Swiss to end one's life expensively and hygienically in Switzerland, was unacceptable on so many levels – aesthetic, philosophical, moral, financial, logistical. Perhaps once Brexit is finally settled (I know, but this is meant to be a funny book), parliament can turn to the much more important, though possibly even thornier matter of – Flexit – the Final Exit.

The talk then reverted to facelifts, neck lifts, bosom implants, tummy tucks and knee lifts as we all sat with our faces in our hands trying to tauten our jawlines while also smoothing out the necks and heaving up the bosoms. "It is like decorating a house," said Camilla. "You can't just do the top floor. Once you do one room, the rest of the house looks like shit and you have to do the whole house, every floor, every room. Even the basement."

"Where do you end it all?" said Giancarla thoughtfully.

Only one answer as far as I was concerned: "Not in Switzerland."

***

A conservative magazine asked me to contribute a few thoughts on my views on voluntary exits, as "it is such an unusual view, probably rooted in Ancient Greece and the deep, pagan past..."

I have always thought that it was not only totally uncontroversial, but also blindingly obvious that the right to end one's life when one wants to is the most fundamental of all rights, if rights do indeed exist. One didn't ask to be born, and if it all goes pear-shaped, one ought to be able to say "I'm outta here". I started researching to unearth the root of this long and noble exit tradition. I was a little surprised to find practically no references anywhere. Starting with Ancient Greece as the conservative magazine had suggested, any acts of suicide seem to have been imposed on citizens by their society. Socrates only volunteered to end his life by drinking a cup of poisonous hemlock under pressure, and in fact, Greeks are a vigorous and life-loving race with a spectacularly low suicide rate. A young and earnest 19th century anthropologist touring the Cyclades in search of ancient customs, visited the island of Sifnos where the inhabitants were extraordinarily long-lived. "How do you deal with the problem of over-population?" he asked curiously. "Oh," came the cheerful response, "It is less of a problem now, but in the old days we just used to push the old people off a cliff." So no voluntary exit strategies there either.

Roman vein-openings in bathtubs and *Hara-kiri*, the Japanese ritual self-disembowelling following a deemed loss of honour, are also not exactly freely chosen departures. My last resort was the traditional Japanese practice of elderly people going up a mountain to die when they feel that they have become a burden on society and "have a low quality of life", as Prof E would say. On closer inspection, this turns out to be *Ubasuteyama* –

something that they are required to do – often protesting vigorously, rather than an exit at a moment of their choice.

I discussed this with an older cousin of mine (aged 65), and suggested that, given the state of the planet, 70 would be a good time to retire. She had recently become a grandmother so pleaded for another five years to see more of her grandchildren, who are, it has to be said, particularly sweet. So 75 it is.

Interestingly, a Japanese sociologist did a recent study of elderly Japanese people and found that, while most of them intended to burden their families for as long as possible, there was a significant preference among females to want to retire to a nursing home rather than be looked after at home. It seems that they trust "The Land of the Setting Sun Home" or "Falling Cherry Blossoms" more than they trust their husbands/sons/daughters-in-law. Perhaps the trauma of (non-voluntary) *Ubasuteyama* lurks deep somewhere inside the female folk memory…

For my part, I am stockpiling Zopiclone with long expiry dates in a secret place. I just hope that Alzheimer's doesn't set in so quickly that I forget where I have stocked them.

We Are All Broke Inside

I was bullied by my daughter into booking an appointment with our local acupuncturist-cum-Chinese-herbal-medicine shop. They were refreshingly uninterested in my medical history ("we can't cure cancer") and focussed on exactly what I wanted them to focus on – my sore shoulders and a pinched nerve in my neck. Lying quietly with the needles in my back, I could not help but overhear a lady checking in at reception. A longer tale of woe has rarely been heard, at least by me.

"I don't complain but the pain is unbearable," said the disembodied voice from behind the wall,

"People keep telling me that I look so young and that there is nothing wrong with me, but I drive to the supermarket and sometimes I cry just at the thought of getting out of the car. I have two knee replacements because the doctor said that I was very young but ought to have them done. I don't complain, but I have good days and bad days, and on the bad days I feel tired and I don't want to take the pills the doctor gives me as I don't like taking medicines. I am not depressed, I am just in pain and tired, so what I need is something for the pain but it is the fibres in my muscles that are inflamed and so pills don't work even though everyone tells me that I look too young to have such pains. My mother had the same thing – she used to complain all the time and we all said, 'but Mummy, you look so young and there is clearly nothing wrong with you,' so it is definitely genetic, and I think her mother had it too and used to say that she had pains everywhere and felt very tired, and my mother used to say to her 'but Mummy...'"

At this point, the receptionist tried to cut in to ask where exactly the pain was. "It is very difficult to explain, it is everywhere, but not all the time, and then I also have a lung condition... it is called somethingorotheritis, and my doctor says that although I am really too young to have it, it is..."

This lasted the entire half hour I lay there, and by the end, I felt deeply grateful that all I had was stage four cancer and not any of the terrible conditions suffered so bravely by this poor woman.

As I paid my bill, I observed to the receptionist that one didn't realise it but, looking out over St Anne's Shopping Mall, probably nine out of the ten people had something terribly wrong with them but invisible to others.

"Yeh," said the Chinese lady taking my credit card, and smiling (as well she might, for she had up-sold me a package of 16 sessions, plus 12 tubs of a dubious-looking mushroom powder to restore balance in fiery individuals like me, with a whispered "Ten pahcen off fo you", for a mere £55 each).

"Yeh, we ah aw broke inside."

It's All Greek to Me

For the last six months I have been dealing with Greek bureaucracy in matters relating to estate planning. Trying to prove that my husband of 32 years is really my husband, is turning out to be a little tricky. We were married in a tiny village church on a small Greek island, only the second couple to do so since the church was restored after the 1953 earthquake. It took the sextant a while to find the register, which hadn't been used since 1980, to pull out the huge, dusty old book, and then to painfully inscribe, "Florian Donald Maria Freiherr von Hirsch, son of Theodore Emil Freiherr von Hirsch and Hertha Freifrau von Hirsch nee Freiin von Perfall, resident of Julian Way, Julian Hill, Harrow on the Hill, Middlesex, United Kingdom," all in Greek letters, which came out something like, *"Flopian Ntonalnt Mapia Fraeichair bon Xirs"* on hard, shiny paper that reminded me of the Jeyes loo-paper at boarding school in the 1970s. Breathing hard and with tongue poking out in concentration, he then moved on to "Ileana Iby Gratsos, daughter of Beatrice Wilhelmina Koerner etc"- which is particularly hard to transcribe into Greek and looks something like *"Mpeatriki Ouilchelmina Kerner"*. Then, following the rule that the sillier the country, the more grandiose the stamps, a veritable blizzard of red wax stamps and stickers and initialling. The solemnity of the occasion was only slightly marred by Florian, who, showing what I should from now on expect from a Bavarian husband, let out a very small fart into the silence (small, but enough to reduce us both into hysterical giggles).

Thirty-two years later, I was told that this still shiny but slightly faded scrap of paper did not look like a serious wedding certificate. The registrar was too bored to say what the problem was other than there was a mistake in the spelling of one of the names, which had degraded to such an extent during the Chinese-whispers process of double transliteration across two alphabets and back, that it was no longer acceptable. She was adamant that she couldn't help, as the only thing worse than boredom for a Greek bureaucrat is having something to do. I would either have to get remarried – first, however, proving that my original marriage had not taken place, which of course they were not prepared to accept despite having rejected the papers – or to petition the various levels of court of appeals to validate the marriage certificate. In other words, at least nine circles of further Dantean bureaucratic obstruction and delay, each one lasting at least a year. Rather amusingly – were one's sense of humour to survive this – the problem turned out not to lie with the long chain of fiendishly barbaric German names that crawled their ponderous way across the page for over three lines. The problem was the "b" in my middle name, "Iby". "B" exists in the Greek alphabet, but sounds like "V", so the Chinese whisperers had, in transliterating it from English to Greek and back to English, renamed me "Ileana Ivy". Clearly not *Flopian Ntonalnt Mapia Fraeixair bon Xirs's* wife of 32 years or *Mpeatriki Ouilchelmina Kerner's* daughter, funnily enough.

Sadly, with the new anti-corruption drive in Greece, it is no longer possible to bung a brown envelope across the table to the public servant intent on doing nothing. He or she remains as under-equipped, under-qualified, unmotivated, uninterested and un-fireable as before, so now the only difference is that nothing ever gets done.

I could see that despite Prof E's best efforts, I was probably not going to live long enough to see through the whole process. Actually, thinking about it, even a healthy person would probably not live long enough.

I have dealt with Greek bureaucracy all my life, as all Greeks do – and some might even say that this is what has given me cancer – but the situation now had reached an apogee of absurdity. The only way to cope was to start swearing. My cousin Maria, who is much more gently bred and raised than I am, was facing similar problems, and even she was starting to use the F word. I now understand that middle-aged, swivel-eyed people shouting and swearing to themselves on the underground or walking along the pavement, gibbering, waving their hands around and saying "fuck," "wanker" etc, are not suffering from Tourette's or drug abuse or alcohol, they are just Greeks trying to figure out how to fulfil some bureaucratic challenge. Give them a wide berth and avoid irritating them any further than they already are, for they are probably at breaking point.

The Return of Ulysses

The Mayor of Ithaca, incumbent during most of my teens and twenties and even my thirties, and a red-in-tooth-and-nail communist, had excellent ties to all the Eastern European and Iron Curtain countries. The Ithaca Cultural Summer Festival, held every summer to great fanfare among the locals and an equal lack of interest among the tourists, always featured Bulgarian Women's Dance Troupes, East German Workers' choirs, Czech mime groups, Polish Trade Union poetry readings and other such exotic delights. As there was nothing else on Ithaca in those days, we were thrilled by these festivities. One year, as teenagers, we went to a concert given by a Greek songstress, famed for her dark and throbbing voice in which she sang all the great hymns of Greek resistance and the underground during the time of the fascist Colonels' rule during the sixties. The Colonels were long gone, but she could still wind up a Greek crowd like nobody's business. We three sisters swayed passionately with the crowd and fervently hummed along, (we didn't know the words), transported by the emotion of the fight for Freedom or Death, ready to die as martyrs.

"Don't be so silly", snapped my mother with uncharacteristic crossness when we tried to tell her how important and thrilling it had been to feel a part of the crowd. She had fled Vienna in 1937 when the mobs were whipped into frenzies and unleashed on the streets, destroying shops and buildings, burning books and forcing Jews to scrub the cobblestoned lanes while being beaten and abused. She had a very different attitude to crowd hysteria than we, her naïve, English-boarding-school-educated daughters and the happy village folk of Ithaca had.

"How can you fall for such stupidity?"

I was suddenly ashamed, and the magic broke into little bits. I have never since been knowingly affected by any groupthink or joined in any mass outpouring of emotion. To this day, I cannot listen to Maria Farandouri singing her resistance songs without revulsion.

There is, however, a sunny side to the lack of seriousness that characterises all Greek public services if you know where to look. One year, as part of the festivities, the mayor decided to stage a re-enactment of the return of Odysseus to Ithaca. The Eastern European cultural dignitaries had been duly invited, Odysseus was a suitably crafty, squinty-eyed and black-ringleted Ithacisian, the homeland was already there under our feet, it only remained to stage the return. Our little wooden *caiki*, a gaily painted, single-masted boat, was requisitioned as the Homeric vessel bearing Odysseus home. The captain – a tough, iron-straight and laconic seaman from Mykonos, who held the soft, chattering and treacherous Ithacisians in very low regard, was finally induced by dint of sheer blackmail on the part of the harbourmaster, to remove the rather non-bronze-age looking flags, lifebelts and dinghy from the boat, but he steadfastly refused to take down his pride and joy – a brand-new satellite aerial. "You touch that, I kill you," were his words to the harbourmaster and mayor, who in a rare moment of unity and good judgement, believed him.

So, twilight fell, the evening star peeped over the hills, and from across the bay, Odysseus embarked on his homeward voyage. The breeze blew softly to the shore, the nymphs in white muslin (whose absence from Homer's Odyssey the mayor had considered an unforgiveable oversight and who, in his opinion, definitely belonged to the story), pranced around on the cabin roof under the nose of the captain, who stood with a wide grin on his face, enjoying the upskirted views. We sat, guests of honour, next to the mayor and the director of the Yugoslav Workers' Theatre Collective to enjoy the spectacle. The wait for Odysseus's return, true to the Homeric original, did go on a bit long, and the village children, who had been seated as a special treat in the front row, got bored of waiting and started to run around, getting louder and wilder and knocking people over.

"*Paidia* [children], please sit down and be quiet." said the mayor in a polite voice, with a quick glance at the Yugoslav Workers' Theatre Collective director. Then, slightly less politely,

"*Paidia*, I said sit down."

Again, no effect. The children continued to pay no attention at all.

Raising his voice, "*Paidia,* will you sit down and stop making such a noise!"

Then, "*PAIDIA,* sit down, I said, and SHUT UP!!"

Finally, he lost it completely, and forgetting all about the Yugoslav director sitting next to him, much to everyone's delight stood up, grabbed a handful of stones and started pelting the kids in fury, shouting at the top of his voice, "*SKATOPAIDIA, KOLOPAIDIA,* SHIT-BRATS, ASSHOLE BRATS, sit the f***k down and shut the f***k up!!!"

The *skatopaidia* and the *kolopaidia* sat the f**k down, shut the f***k up, the breeze blew, Odysseus hove into view, the nymphs danced, and our boat looked very Mycenaean with its row of papier maché shields hung over its sides, in spite of the aerial. Fluttering from the rigging, bright-coloured flags proclaimed leprosy, plague, SOS, engine failure and the Secessionist Republic of the Seven Ionian Islands. The pageant was judged to have been a huge success – by the Ithacisians at any rate, if not by the bemused Yugoslav directors, East German mimes and Hungarian playwrights. We all felt that the earthy side of provincial, Mycenaean Greece had been perfectly represented, exactly as Homer would have wished. Greek public servants at their very best.

4 am

So, it is 4 am, again, and across the country people are sleeping. Well, not middle-aged women obviously, but everyone else. 4 am, the witching hour. Actually, it is not the witching hour, it is the over-heated duvet hour, when you suddenly wake up, gasping and thrashing like a tuna in a net, trying to disentangle your feet from sheet and duvet. Now you are wide awake. What to do?

What you cannot do is go down to the kitchen for a bowl of cereal or snack, as you have been reluctantly persuaded to try intermittent fasting, and if you cannot make it at least five hours through the night without eating, you might as well give up.

You could get up and watch television, but that would take you to 5 am and scupper any chance of falling asleep again. Thoughts pop into your head, as fragile and ephemeral as bubbles, that you had not had time to think during the day… are your work colleagues doing what they are supposed to be doing? Have you forgotten to tell them what you wanted them to do? Perhaps you should make a list. Yes, you can make one in your head. You like lists, but how to remember the list? Can you try to make a mnemonic song out of it? A sort of rap perhaps? It might chase away the thought of that useless Greek civil servant, who squats like an evil toad on a three-foot pile of documents, which won't be touched at the next meeting of the registrar committee unless she pockets €40,000. You certainly have to call that journalist woman, the one wanting copy for a magazine with a deadline of tomorrow – if only you could remember which magazine – what was her name? Perhaps she doesn't have a name otherwise you would certainly remember it. *How can parents not give their children names?* It would not be allowed by Greek civil servants. And, more importantly, how did the competition company manage to place that article about the Greek islands in the *New York Times* when you didn't and you clearly know far more than they do? It was a truly dreadful article that got everything wrong. Perhaps you should write to the *New York Times* and tell them that. Does it mean though that you are losing your touch? Are you getting old and irrelevant? Is your daughter ready to take over the business? What will you do if you retire? Perhaps you could then finally decide what colour curtains you want to hang in her bedroom you have been decorating for over four months – cream, natural, mushroom... talking of mushroom, remember to google "Ganoderma Lucidum" as suggested by the Chinese herbalist, and add to your list of questions for Prof E if there are any contra-indications with immunotherapy. Do you trust the Chinese herbalist who suggested it in fact? Your neck is hurting again after the acupuncture he did, and you have still got 15 sessions you have prepaid. It had better work. Your neck is hurting because you have been savagely digging your fingers into what you think are acupressure points but apparently are your raw nerve. Your neck is also hurting because your pillow is askew, and now your husband has rolled over onto his back and is making little "phhtttt" noises as he breathes out.

Generally speaking, and looking at the big picture, you are glad he is breathing, but perhaps an elbow in the side will make him turn over. His father made noises like that. Are these things genetic? Like male pattern baldness? Will your sons lose their hair early like your father or late like your husband? Will you lose your hair? That reminds you, where is the winter turban that you carefully kept from your last chemo-bald-phase? You could look for it in the morning after doing the things on your list. What were the first things on your list again? Something about New York, oh yes, you are supposed to answer some client in New York, what was their name? Not *another* person whose parents couldn't be bothered to name them. Honestly...

Perhaps read a few pages in your thrilling new Sean Carrol book on Quantum Theory, called... called something or other. You had got up to the chapter about the mystery of unexplained surprise results in measuring the density of dark matter in the universe. What was the surprise again? It was all a little mysterious even before the surprise, and now you can't really remember what the density of the Universe was, or means. You will have to go back a few pages. If you are being honest, you will have to go back more than a few pages, you will have to go back to the beginning of the chapter. OK, alright, the beginning of the book, perhaps even to the book before that... oh, the book before that was a Bavarian murder mystery where the bride may or may not have got bashed with a sausage. Weddings. That reminds me, bloody Greek bureaucracy why can't they accept my wedding certificate? "Phhttt phhtttt, Phhttt phhttt," Great, he has turned onto his back again. Perhaps I should divorce him anyway. Forget this whole marriage certificate malarkey. Bloody Greek bureaucracy.

Where are my earplugs? Grope grope in the dark, oops, there goes my water bottle, and now I have to pee. Fumble fumble, damn, where are my feet, ouch, blind man feeling his way across the dark to the bathroom, turn on light there – oh no, is that my face in the mirror, is that what I look like? God, I need a facelift, or at least some Botox or laser treatment, or those little strings my cousin in Athens was telling me about. Turn off light, grope grope, back to bed. Find pillows, yank duvet and sheet away from husband, roll him back over again, put in earplugs, start on the curtain colour again.... Cream, mushroom, cream, does it matter, dark matter, cream matter, mushroom, cream *and* mushroom, cream and mushroom...

Eventually, with a little luck, you will bore yourself to sleep.

Thanksgiving

Every six months I am scanned to see how my C is behaving. This is the new rhythm to my life. The weeks leading up to the scan can be a time of "scanxiety" for some people – a sort of pre-menstrual tension period – though you haven't seen a hormone in three years thanks to the highly effective daily pills you take. You get a bit tearful and morose, somewhat short-tempered, smart people don't argue with you too much for fear of unleashing the flood gates or getting an earful, or both. Husbands tend to go on business trips then, the dogs put their tails between their legs and extended family choose to postpone their visits for a while. You, of course, are not aware of this. You think you are being totally normal and your usual easy self, until after your scan results, when all of a sudden, you suddenly find yourself energised and happy, like people who live under permanent cloud cover and only realise how grey it was when the sun suddenly breaks through. You bounce out of Prof E's rooms, hugging the first person who speaks to you, and smiling from ear to ear.

One particular time, I had a premonition that the news was going to be bad. I am not an intuitive person, and my gut feelings are invariably wrong, yet this does not stop me from falling into the trap of taking them seriously. The sense of foreboding was exacerbated by spending a little time with one of my oldest girlfriends, P., who had just been diagnosed with a much more drastic and less treatable cancer than mine, which had bought on very untypical feelings of mortality. I put down the uncharacteristic stressing over the minor decoration I had started in the house to a sort of reverse nesting process – leaving everything in good order for a premature departure rather than for an arrival. Sitting with P. during her chemo one day, I mentioned to her case worker that it was a shame P. was having such a hard time making an appointment to get a chemo-port put in, and couldn't she play the cancer card and say that as she had a very aggressive cancer and perhaps not that long to live (she made big eyes at him and nodded enthusiastically to make the point more convincing), could he not bump her up the queue? He looked around the chemo room full of patients with needles stuck in their arms, and said in a loud voice, "No, that won't work as no one in here has long to live". I expected a bomb to go off, but there was no reaction, no one moved or looked up or did anything. Perhaps it was a very bad day at the clinic. I, however, left thinking that, had I been having chemo in that hospital on that day instead of at my usual clinic, I would have heard that I too didn't have long to live. Perhaps no one at my clinic speaks about such things, perhaps no one tells you anything bad there. The US-style company policy mottos that hang everywhere, state with pious solemnity that they aim to treat every human being with compassion and respect. Did that aim, I wondered, extend to not ever saying anything unpleasant? I had always wondered about that anyway. I mean, imagine a medical company saying that their aim was not to treat people with compassion and respect?

As a result of all this, I had been subdued for weeks. I had had my scans wordlessly (for me, anyway), and the next day, which happened to be Thanksgiving, I had an appointment with Prof E to discuss the results. As I entered his room, he didn't look at me but just said,

"Let's see if you are on my list of patients with issues today."

There was a silence as he looked at his list for what seemed like a very long time. I couldn't tell whether it was because he had found me on the list but didn't know what to say. Finally, he said, "Right let's not beat about the bush, I am delighted with your scans, all pristine. You are my model patient and an example of how to live with cancer and not sit around waiting to die."

I started breathing again, vowing never to listen to my gut feelings ever again, and told Prof E, rather timidly, in case he wasn't aware, about my probably not having long to live.

"What nonsense," he said. "But look, even you are allowed a wobble now and then. Listen, you have had a couple of disappointments already, and there will be times when your scans are not pristine and we will need to move onto a new drug, but the good news is that right now we have a fabulous new drug coming up, which is still being trialled and my colleague Dr C, who as you know is the world expert on it, is very excited about it, and after that there will be others, so there is no reason why you can't go on for a very long time."

Prof E knows how to make a girl purr with happiness – or how to make me happy at any rate – talk of new drugs and trials are my happy triggers. In a further burst of munificence, saying "I know you like this sort of thing," he took out a sheet of paper and started drawing diagrams of what the DS-8201 drug does to poor, unsuspecting cancer cells. Utter bliss.

As if the day could be made even more perfect, he then gave me a prescription for some steroids for when I felt like a little help.

"Oh God, no," said my friend Kate when I told her, "Not more steroids, you are going to start moving furniture again."

Of course, Prof E got a huge hug – as did his secretaries, a rather startled new patient waiting outside (Prof E: "Have you met Ileana yet?"), the cleaning lady I met in the lift, and all the nurses down in the chemo suite where I was headed for my treatment.

Life is beautiful. Happy Thanksgiving everyone.

String Theory

I had long felt, even outside of the 4 am window, that something as fascinating as my Greek cousin's bold statement that all my girlfriend's cheeks and jowls were held up by bits of barbed strings, needed further investigation. My friend Grace felt that as well and emailed me one day to say that she had researched the matter very thoroughly and had made an appointment to have a consultation with the leading practitioner of this in London. "This is the doctor who trains all the others, the font of all these minor beauty procedures so to speak. Will you come with me and see what you think?"

Grace is not very jowly at all, far less so than me, but the spirit of journalistic enquiry burns strongly in me, and if someone was volunteering themselves as a guinea pig, so much the better.

I turned up limping and looking like a cartoon tramp, thanks to a boot which had dissolved in the rain and was trailing flapping chunks of rubber heel and sole and shedding black bits with every footstep. Not the impression we wanted to make on the font of all minor beauty procedures.

It was clear from the reception room, however, that this was not the normal kind of Harley St Clinic. First of all, the room was generously scattered with purple marabou feather cushions, and secondly, the receptionist was packed into a minute, black, body-bandage dress which squeezed out her bosom, lips, cheekbones and eye lashes like toothpaste out of a tube, or like some volcanic lava spill, forming a terrifying series of orange, shelf-like structures onto each of which one could probably stand a vase of flowers. Thirdly, there was no coffee machine.

Grace and I tried to avoid making eye contact with each other in case we got the giggles. The apparition did something with her face that could have been a smile and handed Grace a form to fill out. I am used to the forms that ask about medical conditions, but not ones that ask how much filler you have already have, what bits of your body and face are real or not, and whether you are allergic to nylon and silicone. This might have been the Harley St area, but it was not familiar countryside at all. To add to the *Alice in Wonderland* feel, another orange apparition popped her head round the door, with even bigger shelves and fringes sticking out, and said in a husky, Bond-baddie Russian accent, "I am Doctor X," and led us down a narrow staircase to her den. Her black body-bandage dress was even smaller and shorter, her tights had a ladder, her hair extensions were halfway down her head, and her upper lip could hardly move. "I live in Essex," she informed us quite unnecessarily, "We can do the procedure either there or here. It is not cheaper if we do it there, but more expensive if we do it in London. *[No, I have no idea what she meant either.]* In Essex you have more privacy though, after the surgery, no one will see you coming out with bandages all over your face; *shvoop*, into the car, no one is there, while here you come out into, well, Oxford St."

The door then opened again, and in came her assistant, who was the most terrifying of all three; she couldn't even pretend to smile or talk any more. Not that she was going to – my boot was now so thoroughly dissolved that I was leaving black rubbery puddles of grit all over the black and white tiled floor, and her main concern was to cast disapproving looks at this. I tried to hide my feet under the chair, and Grace and I focussed hard on not looking at each other. Grace explained how we had been given her name by a former trainee of hers.

"Never heard of her," said Dr X flatly. "But I have ten thousand people in my database so that means nothing. Perhaps if I see her, I will recognise her."

If the trainee had been "done" like the others, there is no way her own mother would recognize her, and no way Dr X would be able to distinguish her from all the other women she had done either, but we let that pass.

Dr X lectures all over the UK on minor beauty treatments, not just threads, and it was a (non-surgical) eye-opener to hear how much research goes into these things.

"When we are young, our faces are a downward pointing pyramid with cheekbones at the top, broad bit, and ending with a pointed chin. As we get older, the pyramid inverts and everything falls down, so the broad bit is now at the bottom of your face."

Grace and I both sucked in our cheeks.

"People will always look first at your eyes, then at your lips," she continued, her bosom bulging out towards us, straining to escape out of the black dress in a way that rather contradicted what she had just said. "So we can also talk about the bags under your eyes and the tear troughs."

Tear troughs are those sunken furrows above our cheeks that make you look old and tired.

Grace and I both tried to enlarge our eyes, blow air up into our cheeks and purse our lips.

"I can't do anything about your necks," she went on ruthlessly, "Too much skin."

Grace and I stretched our necks as gracefully as we could.

"Here are some 'before and after' photos I can show you," said Dr X, and the assistant pulled out a folder. 'Before' was a tired looking man with bags under his eyes. The 'after' photo showed the same man with no bags, but one eye swivelled left and one eye swivelled right.

"Ooooooh!" cooed Grace who has lovely manners, "That is absolutely fantastic, quite miraculous what you can do with a little filler, don't you think so, Ileana?"

"Umm…" was all I could manage.

Back to threads – Dr X explained that little elastic, barbed nylon and silicone threads are inserted down into your cheeks, and the other ends are then hooked up to the top of your head. They last forever – even the worms don't touch them. "But when you have facelifts, the surgeon can take them out if you want."

"Do the threads give a subtle and natural enough difference that our husbands won't notice them?" we asked. (To be fair, Grace's husband would probably not even notice a face transplant.)

"Yes" said Dr X, who understood what we wanted.

"No" said the assistant, to whom the thought of wanting someone not to notice was incomprehensible.

Then of course, come the jowl lifts, the line fillers, the eyebrow lifts, and so on. The price list was produced, and Grace worried about how she could smuggle those sums onto her credit card, which her husband might well notice even if the facelift escaped him.

"We have a Big Book of Lies," said Dr X helpfully, "which you can also use for explaining the bruises and swelling for the first two weeks. For half price treatments, you can also be a 'before and after' training model – but you may of course get a student who is not very good or hasn't done it before."

"I imagine you have insurance," I said, as politely as possible. "I can't help asking, I am a lawyer."

Dr X's eyes narrowed as much as they could, and took on a steely, slavic glint.

"Of course," she said in a meaningful, James-Bond-baddie sort of way, "As do all my trainees. We have excellent insurance."

We complimented her very sincerely on her obvious passion for the subject, took all the leaflets we could manage, thanked everyone profusely, and made our exit – smearing a snail-trail of glistening, gritty, black-rubber gloop back up the stairs, past the purple marabou cushions, past the orange receptionist, and out into the daylight – where we both decided that really, we didn't need anything done at all. What we needed was to buy me some new boots and have a strong cup of tea.

Thinking about it, one thing that both of us *could* do with is a "memory lift" – a good injection of memory fillers or perhaps some nice memory-cell-promoting collagen implants. After the strong cup of tea and a quick nap chez Grace, I left to go to a concert. "Oh no!" wailed Grace on WhatsApp, "I have lost my bag with everything in it, what a disaster!" "How awful," I whatsapped back, "I am so sorry, and I have lost my beautiful scarf which I left somewhere." After five minutes, my phone pinged again: "It's alright, I found my bag, I was sitting on it."

"Great, "I pinged back, "And my scarf was round my neck the whole time."

Doctor X – anything you can do about that, either in Essex or in London, we will be back, and in my smart new boots, I promise.

Quite naturally, the *nom de plume* that I gave Grace, became the subject of intense speculation among some of my friends. The give-away was apparently that Grace had lovely manners. Sort of sad really that there is only one possible candidate in my entire circle of friends who fits that bill.

"Don't let her do it." begged one friend.

"Of course I won't!" I replied, "But we are going to explore vagina lifts next – in the interest of getting copy for my book. Do you want to join us?" I am still waiting for an answer.

& General Relativity

String Theory would of course not be possible without Einstein's Theory of General Relativity. Einstein once explained it to a pesky journalist in the following way:

"When you sit with a nice girl for two hours, you think it's only a minute, but when you sit on a hot stove for a minute, you think it's two hours."

That explained it almost as well as another time, when a society lady hosting a salon in his honour, breathed,

"Dear Mr Einstein, please do explain your theory to me!" to which Einstein replied,

"It is like this; a blind man once asked a friend what milk looked like. The friend said, "well, milk is white." "Ah," said the blind man, "What is white like?" "A swan is white," said the friend. "And what does a swan look like?" was the next question. The friend held out his arm bent into a graceful swan's neck shape, placed the blind man's hand on it to feel the shape and said, "A swan looks like this." "Ah," said the blind man, "Now I know what milk looks like."

***

I had my own private relativity epiphany when one day I walked into the waiting room of my cardiologist. To my pleasure, I saw Dr H, my GP, whom I had been trying to phone for a while, sitting with two elderly patients of his, who appeared to be around a hundred years old. They were deep in a conversation about cricket. "So, Doctor, do you enjoy cricket?" asked the husband.

"No, not really, not my thing," answered Dr H.

Dr H will not see 70 again but looked like a naughty schoolboy next to them.

"I must tell you about the MCC and the last time I was at Lords," said the husband.

"No," said the wife, poking him quite painfully in the side, "He said he didn't like cricket."

"What's that?"

"HE SAID HE DIDN'T LIKE CRICKET."

Eventually, a lull in the cricketing conversation occurred and I took the opportunity to pull Dr H away and ask him what it was that I had been wanting to talk to him about. "Humph," I heard the husband say, "Just because a pretty girl wants you, orf you go!"

I gawped, then realised that he was talking about me, proving my theory that all is relative. To this charming older gentleman, a middle-aged lady with bags under her eyes, badly in need of the hairdresser and a facelift – or strings at the very least – was "a pretty girl".

"How is your book doing?" asked Dr H. I told him that for a niche book by someone unknown with the word chemotherapy in the title, 2,384 copies sold was considered a respectable number. "You have a lot of competition out there as well," said Dr H kindly.

"Yes, but they are all dying off," I answered happily.

"That's really not funny," said Dr H, sniggering.

Then, the elderly couple were called in to see the cardiologist, Dr H darted back to them, they rose slowly from their seats, and like a pair of very old Galapagos tortoises, each with a walking stick, their intelligent, bony heads protruding from aged carapaces, they moved very, very slowly into the consultant's room, the husband still muttering, "Pretty girl" all the way.

Child's Play

"Just tell them that you are tired and not well, and that *they* should be looking for ways of helping *you*. The idea that they should tell you off for sounding passive aggressive when you do ask for help is just ridiculous." I was talking sternly to my friend Louisa, but how many parents will recognise this and sigh in recognition. It is slightly more complicated for parents with cancer. When you are diagnosed, your main job is to protect your children from panicking or thinking you are going to die. Your duty is to create as normal a life as possible for them. Those lucky enough to have the sort of cancer that allows them to tick along – for years and years ideally, like Louisa, in a strange way fall victim to their own success. They do too good a job of being normal.

Louisa had just moved house and, after eight years of continuous treatment, was beginning to feel a little jaded. Staying bright and strong while trying to navigate the usual – and sometimes unusual – whirlpools of bringing up lively teenagers is a challenge for most people, even without coping with cancer treatment side-effects. Her children were young when she had

111

been diagnosed, but now, like overgrown fledglings, were weekending and holidaying in the nest with their beaks wide open.

"The trouble is, that the more I tell them to do things, the more they tell me that I am a nag and the less they pay attention. I am sure that my having cancer is a stress for them, so I don't want to create a bad atmosphere."

I agreed with her that endless nagging about putting things away, emptying the dishwasher, helping with the cooking, etc was no fun for anyone, and didn't really have any discernible effect in my experience. More importantly, *it missed the point completely*. The point was to take it down a level, to something much more fundamental, namely, that it was time for her to burst the pretty bubble she had created for her family – time to explain to them that, while they knew of course that she was successfully "living with cancer" – they were now old enough to understand that the years of treatment and anxiety had taken their toll on her. Life was fragile, and precarious, and the bubble she had created was just that – a precious bubble that needed taking care of. The point was that it was now their turn to look after her and make sure that she didn't get too tired or stressed. This idea had never occurred to Louisa, which just goes to show that there really is nothing stronger than the mothering instinct, not even that of self-preservation.

As an aside, I noticed to my satisfaction that after sharing Louisa's woes with my own family (who, by the way, have thankfully moved on from thinking that stopping me eating the wrong things is the most important contribution to my survival chances), miraculously, the dogs were fed, the shopping put away, the kitchen cleaned, the recycling removed, the dishwasher emptied, the salad made – albeit with a certain amount of sighing and eye-swivelling and "What's an endive?" and "Do I have to wash it?" and "Danae didn't have to wash her bag of salad" and "So do I have to cut this up as well?" and finally, with a "This is all a bit hectic..." – without my having to say anything at all. I didn't even have to worry about whether saying "X, please do this" is more passive aggressive than "Could you please do this?" (Yes, according to my nesters, but No according to Louisa's.) Even the greasiest washing up got done, and I got off lightly, with only one, "You are robbing me of my childhood, I should be at school on the other side of the ocean, not here, saying this to you..."

With all the counselling that goes on, there ought really to be a workshop for offspring who have grown up with cancerous mothers graduating into adulthood, having to be gently helped into understanding that they have to start putting away the toys of childhood as well as the plates and saucepans, picking up the mops and vacuum cleaners of responsibility, and assume – perhaps earlier than some of their peers, an adult mantle. It might even rub off on fathers who, with a little professional coaching, could possibly figure out that dishes don't get washed unless they get put in the dishwasher, as the top of a dishwasher is a simple surface with no mechanical function whatsoever. In man-speak, it is no good sitting on the ground *next* to the car and waiting for someone to go "Vrrooom vrroooom". Next to the car, on top of the car, or even *somewhere in the vicinity* of the car just isn't going to cut it. If they learn that, they could then move on to Advanced Level – learning to say whole sentences like, "Supper is at eight, why don't you go and relax and I will cook", rather than "What time is dinner?" and then adding in hurt tones when you snap at them, that they were only trying to be helpful and were asking so that they knew whether they had time for a bath before supper or would just read their book.

To be honest, it is all my fault, as my children never fail to point out.

"You have, by letting Daddy get away with playing the half-wit in the kitchen, simply standing around looking dopey, infantilised him. He will never learn if you do everything for him rather than make him do it himself."

I did catch myself one day, exasperated by his inability to open a black dustbin liner, about to say, "Honestly darling, if you carry on like that, you will never find a woman to marry you", and then realised that I was that woman.

I am being too harsh perhaps, and have to say here that I am exceptionally lucky to have my Old School Bavarian Gentleman, who sometimes sees that I am making supper, but that I am tired and need some help, so starts pulling elderly cabbage halves out of the larder saying, "Perhaps you ought to do something with these as well." For small blessings we should always be truly thankful, and as he also checks my company accounts for me, deals with my health insurance and is my rock, his account is firmly in the black. The dishwasher is also a useful measure of how well my family are coping with having a cancerous mother; if I come down to breakfast and it is all clean and unloaded, they are clearly worried, while the sign of a happily dirty dishwasher means that all is well in their world.

Neurologist

"This doesn't really hurt, just a mild tingling and tapping perhaps," said the kindly-looking, grey-bearded Aussie doctor who was about to test how conductive my nerves were. I had been whining a little too much about having sore legs and had been dispatched off to have some neuro-transmitter electric-current tests done. Little wire rings are slid over your fingers and electrodes patched onto your ankles. A thin needle is then inserted into a calf muscle. It is like sticking all your fingers and toes into a live socket without being allowed to hastily pull them out. After a few goes at this, with me squealing like a pig, and shouting, "Take that thing off now", and "I will scream until you stop!" and finally, "Enough or I will kick you!" Brian finally stopped. Actually, he said, he had done the absolute minimum, taken all the short cuts he could, he hoped that I hadn't scared away his next patients, and that an 85-year-old lady had recently kicked him hard in the face when he tested her knee reflex. He removed all the paraphernalia, adding in a cheery voice, "Well, the good news is that your nerves seem to be conducting signals extremely efficiently." Clearly, I would be no good under torture. When I said this to him. Brian, suddenly serious, turned towards me and taking off his glasses, said "If you ever are tortured, the best thing to do is to wildly over-exaggerate the pain so they think you can't stand anymore." For a split second, he looked less like an Antipodean Father Christmas and more like a semi-retired CIA operative.

"I knew that," I muttered to him in a faint attempt at bravado, "That didn't really hurt at all." Then I fled before he could start again.

Adding insult to injury, in Brian's letter to Prof E, his suggested diagnosis hurt almost as much as his electrodes. "It is possible that Ileana's symptoms are due to Restless Leg Syndrome and could be alleviated with Potassium supplements."

"Restless Legs?" I felt like shouting after I had googled Restless Leg Syndrome. "Potassium supplements? Like eating more bananas? Are you serious? I feel like the Tin Man in *The Wizard of Oz* – all rusted from being left out in the rain – I need taking apart, scraping and oiling, every movement feels as if I am tearing my tin joints apart, and you call it *restless legs*? That is something people write in to "Ask the Doctor" articles in tabloid newspapers. *Dear Doctor, whenever I lie in bed, my legs start to get restless, one wants to grow its hair and have a gap year in South America while the other wants to go off on its own for a bit and get away from the rat race... Does anyone else ever experience this strange symptom?* Good grief, man, go back to water-boarding Isis terrorists. So that was that, and it was back to Ibuprofen. In the end, Google had a much more satisfactory explanation called *myalgia* (Greek for "it hurts"), which was considerably more dignified, though still as painful. Prof E very kindly upgraded it to *arthro-fibromyalgia*, which is Greek for "the bones and fibres hurt", so pride was finally restored.

The Christmas Turtle

My friend Alma was frazzled. Her mother and stepfather, who had been living in Egypt, and descended on Alma for lunch once a year like slightly erratic birds of passage, were back in London. A kind neighbour in Egypt had called Alma to confide that it might be wise to meet them at the airport as they seemed a little confused, which Alma did. Alma's mother was in fact seriously confused and living deep in Dementialand – a parallel world much stranger and lonelier than Cancerland. Alma had spent a fraught few months trying to sort out the muddles and mess that had washed over them all like a tsunami – and I felt for her. My father (and we) had suffered from Alzheimer's for many years, one tried to laugh as much as one could, but the pre-diagnosis state of perennial searching for gloves, keys, glasses, wallet, car, children, tickets, our mother, passports, letters and so on was just the innocent warm-up period that fooled most people into thinking that it was just old age creeping up.

There was the time my father first met Florian, a newish boyfriend then, carefully looked him up and down, which took a few seconds as Florian towered a good head or two over him, then, turning away, announced to all in perfect German, "Unnecessarily tall," and thereafter lost all interest. We still say that to Florian when he gets a bit full of himself. Having been anti-German since the war, as many Greeks of his age were, my father coped with my having a German boyfriend by deciding in his mind that as the surname began with "H" and there was a title, he must be a Hapsburg, and therefore not only acceptable, but all in all, quite a catch for a humble girl from Ithaca. "Darling," he would say to me, "You will one day be the most important woman in Europe, but never forget where you come from!" "No, Daddy," I would promise him, "I won't."

Or the time he dismissed a handsome Greek friend of ours – who was sporting a dreadful moustache nicknamed "the Slug" that no one could persuade him to shave off – with a disapproving "too much hair" before walking away. That was the end of the Slug. The time he came across my one-year-old son playing quietly in my bedroom, inspected him with interest for a minute or two, before looking around and asking, "Who left the dwarf here?"

Then there was the time he tried to make a "nice cuppotee" as he called it in his Greek-accented English, for my mother, who was dealing with breast cancer at the time, (how did she do it all? I now wonder), by dropping a tea bag in the kitchen sink, putting in the plug and running the hot water tap. The times he would call the local taxi company to take him to Geneva – we had an arrangement whereby they would drive him around Harrow on the Hill and deliver him home again. The time he carefully broke a large gilt mirror hanging in the hall into tiny little bits and hid every last piece in the garden. The time that he invited two rather startled young Jehovah's Witnesses into the house when they rang the bell and asked him if he was interested in saving his soul. He wouldn't let them go until he had showed them every last book in his – extensive – antiquarian book collection and had cried copious tears over the beauty of the Greek Orthodox ritual, telling us afterwards that he had had *such* nice people over for tea (they never came back again).

My brother-in-law, who lives in Hollywood and was a very handsome and accomplished actor, didn't visit that often, but the last time he did, my father never quite got the hang of who he was. Every day was different, one day Gene was the plumber, the next day the piano tuner. Gene, to his credit, played each role beautifully, though I am not sure how well Stanislavsky's Method Acting classes could prepare someone for, "You are the dishwasher repair man who is being shown an antiquarian book collection by a bearded old man in a dressing gown – in German." or "You are the electrician who is being told about Greek Orthodox church ritual and the beauties of Christianity by a tearful old man who thinks you have come to tune the piano." Anyway, Gene carried it all off with great aplomb.

There was the time my father had taken up a walking stick and chased away a well-meaning psychiatrist who had come to assess him, causing him to flee for his life back down the drive. His crime? To have rung the doorbell and greeted my father with an "Ah, you must be the Armenian gentleman I am visiting!" Armenians being only marginally better than Turks, though better than Germans.

In fact, the psychiatrist fled so quickly that he left his briefcase in the porch. "What a peculiar man!" said my mother watching him depart, who, having been married to my father, knew a fair bit about peculiar men. She then opened the briefcase to see to whom it ought to be returned, exploded with laughter and rushed to the nearest loo, returning a few minutes later to explain herself. "His name is Dr Weir but I misread it as Dr Weird!"

"Fertile ground," said my friend John when I told him I was writing about Alzheimer's. "It brings back so many memories of parental dementia. I have my mother's tombstone setting ritual tomorrow, which will revisit so much of the past – in particular my mother's last words to me, telling me how pleased she was I'd been released from jail. In fact what I had told her was that I had been staying with friends in Greece, which must have got lost in translation. One of my favourites was when she described a couple saying, 'they're so bohemian – they have breakfast when they wake up.' Or when she wanted to say to someone that the future was in their genes, but it came out "the future is in your genitals." She could never even master names pre-dementia. My brother had a girlfriend called Koti who'd defected from Hungary. Mother created her own mnemonic to remember Koti's name which never worked. She'd ask David: "How's the Hungarian defective?"

Non-demented mothers also present challenges: my friend Cathryn's mother was a *grande dame* - the epicentre of an extraordinarily explosive, complicated, extended family clan of raving eccentrics, including my friend Cathryn. Cathryn's mother didn't have Alzheimer's, but simply grew more outlandish and took secret delight in identifying everyone's weak points and then triggering them, hard. Tom and Cathryn had her to stay for three months when she needed a little extra care, and one day, towards the end of her stay, over lunch, she finally managed to break Tom.

"Would you like some more wine?" he had asked her politely.

"Yes," said Cathryn's mother.

"Yes, what?" asked Tom, who had decided that after three months he deserved a 'please' or a 'thank you,' just once.

"Yes," she repeated.

"I am sorry, what did you say?" asked Tom,

"YES!" repeated Cathryn's mother, a little louder.

"Yes, *what?*" he tried again.

Cathryn's mother just looked at him, then turned to her daughter,

"Cathryn, darling," she said, "Is Tom DEAF?"

So, back to the main story. Alma's mother had, on her return to London, for some reason – although she had never shown any interest in antiques before her visit – decided that she in fact worked as front-of-house in a second-hand furniture shop in Shepherd's Bush, into which she had wandered one day, and to which she now turned up every morning punctually for work.

After a while, the good souls of the shop that I shall call Abingdon Antiques, bowed to the inevitable and set out a chair for her, and there she sat every day in her fur coat, happy as a clam, smiling benignly at the customers and delivery men who came in and out.

"That," said Alma, "Is what I call 'Care in the Community'."

We both felt that Abingdon Antiques deserved a grant, and perhaps an emergency number, should Alma's mother decide at some point that she was also the electrician.

A few days before Christmas, my fourth one since diagnosis – by which time I had perfected a low-key celebration – I did sense that something was missing. As my late father-in-law once memorably expressed his views on religious rituals; they were "turtle soup without the turtle," nutritious and enjoyable, but no turtle.

Then Alma emailed me to say that her mother was still bubbling over with excitement following last night's Abingdon Antiques's Christmas party, to which the angelic shop-owners had invited her as one of the staff. And behold! The turtle suddenly materialised in the soup and Glory shone around.

When I shared this story the next day with my clinic nurses during my pre-Christmas treatment, one of them, who had worked with Alzheimer patients before, said, "Oh that is so lovely, that made my day, I will smile whenever I think of it." So, on behalf of the LOC nurses and myself, thank you Abingdon Antiques for giving Alma's mother a front of house position and asking her to the Christmas party, and thank you Alma, for allowing me to share your precious story.

Turtle or no turtle, that year was the year we finally cracked Christmas. My family are, to a man, Christmas depressives. They hide in dark corners radiating discomfort and dread, while I rush around in desperation festooning anything that doesn't move with trails of ivy and startled spiders from the garden, singing "Silent night" and "We Three Kings of Orient Are," in a manic way, in order to generate festive spirit, while swearing never to do it again. This year, fatigue, the inability of my family to plan ahead, and most of all, the memory of the mountains of *stuff* that I had fought to throw into the skip and had only just succeeded in clearing, meant that we agreed on a minimal Christmas. A candlelit crib, a small tree with roots (for the Eco Warrior) some old videos (rescued from the aforementioned skip by the Eco Warrior), and *no presents at all.* The trash and tinsel of London, which had started this year even before Halloween, simply washed over us. We looked pityingly at people lugging bags and parcels and wearing Christmas sweaters of unrecyclable polyester, shop windows were seen for what they really were – child-labour tat and yet more wasted resources (oh dear, the Eco Warrior is beginning to have an effect on me), and I have to say, it was the happiest Christmas ever. The Depressives started smiling one by one, like shy, night-blooming flowers beginning to unfurl their petals as they realised that it was all going to be alright, I didn't have to sing Silent Night, the spiders rested easy in the ivy, and we agreed to do exactly the same next year.

It was miles better at any rate than Christmas chez my Danish friend Tina, who has been an eco-hippy since I first met her 40 years ago when we were both working as scenic artists in New York. She donated a goat to a Sudanese farmer in the name of her 92-year-old father, and then spent the next three days explaining to him why the goat was nowhere to be seen, how it came to be in the Sudan rather than his Danish homestead, and why, in spite of that, it was such a brilliant present.

"*Ja,* Tina, this card says that you have given me a goat. I don't see a goat, where is it?"

"In the Sudan, Papa, helping to support a local farming community."

"But how did it get to the Sudan from here?"

"It didn't Papa, it was never here, it was already in the Sudan."

"Why did you give me a goat that was in the Sudan, when there are plenty of goats in Denmark you could have given me?"

"Papa, the point is that the little farmer in Sudan needs a goat and you don't."

"So why did you buy me a goat at all if I don't need one?"

"It is your present to a farmer in the Sudan!"

"But I don't know any farmers in the Sudan, and even though you gave me a present that I don't need, why have you given it to someone I don't know without asking me?"

"But Papa, you didn't really want a goat, did you?

120

"No, and as you already knew that, why give me something I don't want? Where is my real present?"

"The goat, Papa, I have explained this to you already."

"But I don't see any goat..."

Three days of festive wind-up. He must have loved it. I think Tina will come round to my way of thinking next year.

I mentioned this to a Vancouver cousin of mine, whose comment was "This year, our Christmas goat was a greenhouse we gave to a First Nation Nunavit family for food security, as it is just as hard to grow things in the cold as it is in the heat."

Luckily, she only has a grown-up child to explain that to.

I can just imagine Tina's father...

"Tina, what do you mean the Christmas goat is a greenhouse? And why is the greenhouse you gave me in Nunavit? Where is Nunavit? I don't understand what is happening. I would quite like a greenhouse here, not in Nunavit. Somewhere to put the goat you didn't give me last Christmas. Next year, perhaps you could just give me a pair of socks or a polyester Christmas sweater, or, if it has to be recyclable, a bottle of Akvavit is also fine."

***

If my family are Christmas depressives, I am a New Year's Eve one. This has nothing to do with any pressure one might feel to have been invited to a fabulous party or a black-tie gala performance of Die Fledermaus with chauffeured limousine waiting to drive one home at the end, but it has everything to do with my tendency to prefer the devil we know to the one we don't. I am totally aghast at the appalling lack of gratitude we display to the old year gone by. We chase it away with bangs, flashes and shouts, just to welcome in a completely unknown New Year. Come on people, the old year kept us alive (those of us who are celebrating anyway). No matter how difficult it may have been, you are still here, as is the world. You have absolutely no idea on the other hand, what the New Year will bring. It could be global catastrophe, it could be your demise, it could be the worst year of your life. The fickleness of humans fills me with dismay. We should have thanksgiving services for the Old Year, and wave it away respectfully, with grace and thanks, and above all, no rude and unseemly haste to replace it with a stranger who has, as yet, done nothing for us. Suspicion is what I greet every New Year with. I understand that one needs to propitiate a potentially maleficent New Year with a show of enthusiasm and excitement, but if it catches sight of how churlishly we will shuffle it off once it is 12 months old, you can let off as many fireworks and pop as many champagne corks as you want, but in my view, it is all wasted effort. My thoughts at midnight are entirely ones of gratitude to the year that has allowed so many of my loved ones, friends and family – and Prof E and myself of course – to survive. One should really pay one's respects and bring flowers to a little grave, "Here lies the Old Year, RIP" every January 1st. And if the New Year proves to be an improvement on the old one, then I will celebrate the next New Year's Eve with even less enthusiasm. As this was written on the 31st of December 2019, I feel that my point was well made and very timely, though 2020 will be saluted just as respectfully on its demise as 2019 had been. One never knows.

Cathryn (she of the mother who would not say "please"), came to sit with me for the TLC a week after New Year's Eve. She arrived looking like an elegant bag lady with what looked like pyjama bottoms under a dress and a bursting bag of groceries that trailed bits and pieces, like a snail moving house. "I am surprised they let you in," I commented, "They don't usually allow people looking like you to enter clinical spaces." Then we started to compare New Year's Eve notes. Her husband, Tom, an action man if there ever was one, was suffering from two knackered knees and was unhappily immobilised, so both of them had tried to ignore the whole New Year's Eve thing. It had, she said, been so awful that it was in the end funny, though Cathryn's sense of humour is even stranger than mine. "Honestly," she said, "Tom has been a huge baby – he is a total hypochondriac. Just because he has a deep vein thrombosis and is taking blood thinners, he grumbles that he can't take pain-killers for his knees and is making the most frightful fuss." If it has four legs, Cathryn is an angel, a Florence Nightingale, a Mother Theresa – but unless Tom grows another two legs, and ideally a mane, he is out of luck. Tracey the chemo nurse, who was fiddling with my IV drip, said to Cathryn, "I do sympathise, I would much rather be taking care of animals than people. I really wanted to be a vet, not a nurse, but my mother said that she forbade it as the house would be full of stray dogs and three-legged cats in just a few days. I just don't feel that way about people." She and Cathryn looked at each other adoringly while I kept a wary eye on the large hypodermic needle that Tracey was waving around. Then Cathryn continued, "Anyway, to make up for being such a misery, Tom had booked a table for New Year's Eve in the local pub, can you imagine! I said 'No, I refuse to go to the horrible "Puddle and Cowpat" for New Year's Eve, so he then hobbled into the kitchen on his crutches and made the most inedible supper ever. I mean, really. I said, 'Tom, I refuse to eat that' so we went to bed."

"You are absolutely horrible and don't deserve a nice husband like Tom," I said, "But my poor family didn't fare any better. I thought I would make *vitello tonnato*," (that elegant Italian dish of cold, perfectly roasted veal, sliced thin and blanketed with a delicate, pale sauce of tuna, capers and mayonnaise), "But I forgot to roast the veal the day before, so had to slice it while it was hot, and of course it was all huge, thick, uneven slabs of wobbly, fatty meat that fell apart and haemorrhaged blood all over the place which congealed on the plate. I tried to hide it all under the sauce, but no one was fooled. It was disgusting. The children scraped the sauce off, which they ate with bread, while Florian shouted at them that no one could expect him to eat that meat without the sauce, so in the end we threw it out of the window and the fox ate it." We agreed that it was a good job we all had a year to recuperate and moved on to discussing Cathryn's vast network of cousins, half-siblings, half-cousins, step-cousins, step-siblings and whatnots.

"He brought his mother who surprised us all by saying in church on Boxing Day that she was a lay priest. Very attention-seeking we all felt."

"I can imagine, but who is 'he'?"

"Ed."

"How should I know that 'he' means Ed?"

"I didn't say 'he', I said Ed."

"Well, who is Ed then?"

"Ed is Jane's boyfriend." I didn't ask who Jane was at that point...

"And why did Ed's mother say she was a lay priest?"

"Because the vicar was late, so she got up and preached instead. We gained incredible kudos in the village."

Conversing with Cathryn is an art form.

Cathryn then moved on; "Poor Amelia," she said in a loud, clear voice, "Her daughter has gone to Spain to learn hoeing." The clinic fell silent.

"Hoeing?" I asked faintly, "Are you sure?"

"Yes, hoeing and weeding, she wants to start a farm for inner-city children to visit."

The clinic breathed again. "Cathryn," I said, "I am sure it is fine in the West Country to say that, but in the wider world, you can't really say 'hoeing' anymore, it means something quite different."

Luckily, she had a train to catch, and as there were no more urgent revelations about her extended family, she gathered her bags and skirts together and left, and the room suddenly seemed dimmer, as if the lights had gone out.

The Thin End of the Wedge

The New Year did kick off in a rather strange way as it happened (though in hindsight, nothing compared to how 2020 developed after that...). A tiny crack appeared in my carefully constructed carapace of superficiality and stunted spirituality. Spending time with my new-age-ish daughter is probably to blame. We spent New Year in the rather run-down and hopeless little Italian ski resort in the Dolomites, where we go quite often. The best thing about the place is that despite the stupendous beauty of the pinnacles of rock that thrust up into the sky and stand guardian over the valleys, the village is so hopeless that it attracts almost no skiers, even over the festive season, just families with small children, sleds, picnics and a truly astonishing array of dogs, who all dress up with snow-shoes, rucksacks and walking sticks as if they were crossing the Himalayas (the families, not the dogs, though quite often, the poor mutts skulk around looking mortified in booties and a knock-off Burberry coat). Then they (the families), stroll with tremendous noise and chat for all of three kilometres to a nearby *ristorante*, where they spend the rest of the day sunk in deckchairs with their faces turned to the sun, while the children happily sled and the dogs wind their leads around every human or chair leg while being fed scraps of bresaola and *Sachertorte* with *panna montata*, and trying to mount each other through the Burberry coats (the dogs, not the families). The glittering snowfields and glowing sunset peaks are left for us to enjoy all on our own. The cliffs fringe the distant horizon in curtains of pleated and folded bronze, a parade of splendour that marches down and surrounds the valley like remnants of an ancient wall, and one can almost feel the energy ringing out as the vibrations bounce from rock to rock, spire to spire, pinnacle to pinnacle, while the blue air contained within, shimmers and pulses with light. Having felt not very well for most of the autumn, and even caught myself feeling a bit despondent and depressed, I was ecstatic to discover that being up in the mountains immediately filled me with energy, and from having worried about whether I would cope with even walking let alone skiing, I felt like my old self again.

"One might almost say," said Danae in a casual sort of way, "That the dolomite rock has a healing effect, no?" I had to agree.

"In fact," she went on relentlessly, homing in on the opportunity, "You might almost agree with me that rocks contain energy, and that well-chosen ones can strengthen our energy fields." Again, I said that she had a point.

"So perhaps you might now take my crystals a little more seriously in future and open your mind to their healing vibrations and to my other non-traditional suggestions and stop thinking that I am a new-age flake."

I could almost hear the cracking noise as my tectonic plates shifted a little. Once that starts to happen, once the thin end of the wedge is in place, who knows what natural disasters burst up through the cracks – geysers, volcanic eruptions, tsunamis, earthquakes, sinkholes, meditation, astrology, Tibetan gong-healing, colour therapy, aura whisperers – I just hope that back in London, the plates settle down, even though the memories of

125

the rock-flung vibrations remain, quietly vibrating with raw, mineral energy.

I did walk every evening in the fading light, up to where the snow ended and the pinnacles burned luminous in the last sunrays, and as a half-moon and Venus swam around each other in the twilight air, I listened to the sound of the healing vibrations echoing from rock to rock, and felt well again.

Gender Fluids

Perhaps I spend more time than most in public lavatories, what with hospitals and clinics, so finding them objects of fascination is not as unusual as it might appear. The British Museum and various clinic loos have already been mentioned. At the other end of the scale is the Ladies on the top floor restaurant of the Shard – the twinkling lights of London, the river boats and bridges, the London Eye – all spread out before you as you sit enthroned, with purple and blue lighting tastefully bathing the walls. The prize for the most baffling bathroom was won by a *rifugio* in a little ski resort in Italy, where the pictures which normally show which is the *Signore* and which the *Signori,* were placed side by side on the same door. One showed a hirsute alpine type, a sort of *Oetzi* in lederhosen, wearing a big grin and his hat set at a jaunty angle, very definitely male – but the other, where one would normally expect a buxom lady busting out of a dirndl, was a gracefully swaying androgynous figure with bobbed hair and tapered ski-pants. No sign of a dirndl dress anywhere. An Italian man and I stood in front of this in consternation. He clearly wondered if the sign meant heterosexuals and transgender, or men and women, and didn't want to be mistaken for a transsexual or barge into a room full of Italian mammas either. I didn't care either way, I just didn't want to share facilities with a lot of people who pee standing up, however they identify, simply for hygiene reasons. There seemed to be no alternative. We stood there with crossed legs for a while blinking at each other, then he said in desperation, "These are mixed facilities", and headed for a corner cubicle, while I headed for one that had a light and loo paper, where the androgynous-type might have been the previous occupant, rather than *Oetzi*.

The ski-resort that we went to a few days later was an altogether smarter affair, with shiny new chairlifts that whisked you up in groups of six in seconds, and quality control that extended to every aspect. There, rather than the cracked, porcelain-edged holes in the ground of our usual skiing place, the loos seemed to have been bought in a job lot along with the chairlifts and designed by the same person. As you approached, the seat lowered itself onto the base, then you sat down, and after a period of time (which was not of your choosing), the seat suddenly lifted, the water flushed, and you were ejected. At least these were single seaters, not six seaters, for which one must be grateful.

Those who design taps, sinks and soap dispensers seem to challenge themselves to make everything as invisible as possible. This results in some extraordinarily poetic scenes of women who stand like ballerinas rehearsing in front of the mirror, slowly and gracefully waving their hands around in the vicinity of where a tap or soap dispenser might be, in figures of eight, up and down, in and out – rather like Tai Ch'i. If after five minutes of fruitless waving of limbs you give up, say "Oh sod this!" and walk out without washing your hands, you would then be immediately branded as filthy. Every woman in there wants to give up but doesn't dare as every other woman is also watching like a hawk for someone to crack. Finally, one especially persistent, agile or experienced woman will stumble upon the code, obtain water or soap or hot air, and everyone heaves a sigh of relief, pretends to do the same thing, ostentatiously flapping hands in a fraudulent attempt to dry that which never got wet, and leaves. Men couldn't care less, and if it doesn't work straight away, just walk out humming.

"You have to stop writing things like that!" exclaimed my children in horror on reading this, but public lavatories have not yet had their Mark Twain or Proust, so perhaps it is time for them to be brought out into the open and given an airing, so to speak.

The lowest to which one could ever sink in the collection of twentieth century European facilities were the loos in the Athens central bus station. Right up until the new millennium, the

127

infamous KTEL was a dreaded pit of diesel fumes, feral pigeons and unidentified piles of things lying around steaming. The only upside was the signs that announced that the 12.25 to Drama was leaving from platform two, or that the 11.45 to Metamorphosis had been cancelled. *Madame Pipi,* as the French call the lavatory attendants, handed out tiny squares of thin, grey, crackly paper in exchange for a tip, while you entered on tiptoe and squatted gingerly trying not to touch anything at all. Through the throngs of travellers wandered beautiful, unbelievably dirty gypsy women, selling packets of tissues, while their huge-eyed offspring expertly relieved the unwary of wallets. All very nineteenth century Balkans, with echoes of the early Baedeker guidebooks to the Ottoman Empire, the ones which would advise travellers to bring collapsible rubber baths and pictures of Queen Victoria to hand out to the locals.

The gypsies were artists and entertainers of the highest order. On one particular visit to the KTEL, as I waited for a couple of boring hours to pass before the ferry to Ithaca left, a dark-eyed gypsy woman approached me; "You have a beautiful soul and a good heart," was her opening. Well, who could resist such honesty and perception? "But," she continued, "You have a pain in your heart. Would you pay 20 euros for me to remove it?"

I was bored, there was nothing else to do, so I said I would.

"Good. Give me a 20 euro note, I will fold it up small, place it in your bra, you put your hand over it, and I will cast a magic spell and drive out the pain."

I looked in my wallet but could only find a 50 euro note. "Will that do?" I asked. Her eyes lit up, clearly unable to believe her luck in finding such a cretin. "I can make that work," she said casually, folded it up small and handed it to me, telling me to put it in my bra and keep my hand over it. I did as she said. She then muttered away exotically for a few minutes and said, "Now look and see if the note is still there." It wasn't. Melted into thin air although my hand had not moved an inch. "It worked!" she cried dramatically, "Your pain will be gone now!"

"But what happened to the 50 euros?" I asked.

"What are you complaining about?" she asked, "Isn't it worth that to get rid of your pain?"

She was of course totally right, it felt churlish to ask for 30 euros change, so I thanked her and felt that she had earned every penny. You don't get that sort of personalised service now, and travel is the poorer for it. I blame the EU. Not even the gypsies want to work in Greece anymore.

***

On the subject of gender, in lavatories or elsewhere, all I can say as to whether or not there exist objective differences, is that at an airport security queue, you should never choose the line with more men than women. I am constantly astounded by men in a security check line-up. This is, I imagine, what goes through their heads when they get dressed the morning of a flight:

"I am flying today, what would be a suitable outfit given that I have to pass through a metal detecting security check which obliges me to empty pockets, remove belts and also to take off all external layers of clothing? Hmmm, let's see, choose a belt. This one is really hard to get out of the trouser loops. Yes, that's good. Then it would be as well to add a pair of braces, just in case my trousers fall down once the belt is off. Now, which trousers? Jeans I think, they have about six pockets into which I can strew lots of small change, and a couple of pockets that are too small for me to really get my fingers into to retrieve the small change when it is time to put it in the tray. OK, Jeans, check, belt, check, braces, check.

Now for the socks. Those ones on the floor are a few weeks old and have huge holes in them – but no one is going to see them, and I wouldn't dream of taking my boots off on the plane. Boots, yes, thick soles with lots of laces and perhaps a double knot to make sure they don't come untied. While I am at it, a treble knot.

What next? A safari vest with lots of very macho-looking and useful compartments so I can carry my mobile, watch, bracelet, sunglasses, some old Deutschmarks just in case, a keyring, yes, those can all get packed down on top of the extra small change I can now fit in. Right, that's the under-layer. Now I can put a sweater on top, a jacket over that, with a few more pockets filled with biros, keys, a magnet (you never know), a mini screwdriver

129

(be prepared!), a couple of loose batteries, a calculator, my car keys, house keys, nail clippers and maybe a hip flask. And my wallet of course. Then my passport and boarding card need to go into a separate pocket as well. Done.

Now what is left? A scarf, headphones, a hat, a bum bag with three separate compartments for foreign change and an anorak with a few more pockets. Yup, that should do the trick. My laptop, iPad, iPod, console, chargers etc can all go, along with my one litre bottle of water in a re-useable metal canister, into my backpack, the one with seven different compartments which all zip up and has at least 20 straps, and of course I really ought to padlock it all and stow the key somewhere safe... Good to go!"

Then, at the airport, where the queue folds up and down the aisle at least four times, they shuffle along slowly, steaming in all their layers, until: "Oh, my word, am I at the counter already? Wow, who would have guessed, that went by fast, and there I was staring into space listening to my reggaeton and chillin'. The security guy is saying something to me... let me take my headphones off so I can hear him. Ah, they want me to take off my headphones. Yup, can do that, cool. Oh, he is saying something else. I have to take off my boots, coats, jacket, scarf, hat, vest, sweater, put each gadget in a separate tray, decant my water into a 30-millilitre bottle and seal it in a small clear plastic bag. Oh, how funny, there are descriptions and pictures of people doing just that all over the hall! What a coincidence! Laptop and camera out of the small backpack and the small backpack out of the larger backpack? OK, OK, no problem, sounds reasonable to me. Now, where did I put that padlock key?"

"Honestly," I usually hiss to my husband when behind one of these types, "Men..."

"What's wrong with men?" asks my husband in surprise as he slowly unbuckles his belt and starts fishing ten cent coins out of his jeans' pockets.

Perhaps it all comes down to *Oetzi*-types not having little handbags – but until they do so, we really need a separate line for them. I know some pretty good icons that could be used.

Bitter Oranges

Age is a recurring theme, probably because it did not gradually creep up on me, but was chemically induced almost overnight. As a result, I am still examining it as a phenomenon and trying out the different approaches to having a successful relationship with it. We have ruled out strings and face-lifts for now, we have discovered that charm and beauty are relative, and if beauty is in the eye of the beholder, the rheumier the eye that is beholding, the better, so progress is being made.

I also learned however, that although some bits age, i.e. knee joints, memory and eyesight, other bits don't change at all.

On a sunny winter's morning in Athens not long ago, I was sitting on a balcony in an old part of town, overlooking a quiet and narrow road on the edge of Mount Lykabettus lined with bitter orange trees in full fruit, and enjoying being thoroughly in the moment. Somewhere below, an accordion started playing, and an old man wandered into sight, singing a lovely old *cantada*, one of Greece's beautiful traditional songs, about love, longing and the passing of time. "I love you," he warbled as he walked along, squeezing plangent chords out of his accordion, "Because you are good". A few residents tossed the odd coin down into the street for him. I leaned over the balustrade to hear him better, still in my white nightgown, and he looked up, singing to me, and for a moment, we were a couple of geriatric Romeo and Juliets.

I opened my purse to find some coins, but had only a five euro and a ten euro note.

"Can I throw you down a note?" I called to him.

"Yes, throw it down," he called back.

I took careful aim, adjusted the trajectory for the breeze, and down fluttered the five euro note, only to land on top of one of the bitter orange trees.

"Now what am I supposed to do?" he complained. A couple of workmen nearby came over to help him shake the tree, another tried to reach it on the ladder. Nothing. After several minutes of fruitless attempts, almost in tears, he resumed his forlorn way down the road. I nearly cried too. There was nothing for it but to try again. This time, all I had left was the ten euro note, which I stuffed in a plastic bottle, called him to come back, and chucked the bottle down to him. He picked up the bottle on the bounce, a beam split his face in two, he put his hand on his heart and sang just to me, as I stood above the bitter orange trees in the morning sun, in my white nightdress. Then he bowed and wandered off on his chosen path again.

"That five euros is going to flutter down from the tree at some point," said my friend to whom I told the story, "And some child catching it will turn to his father and say, 'You see, money *does* grow on trees.'"

The touching romance of the serenade and the old man's smile stayed with me all day. I never spent 15 euros more wisely.

***

I have learned that even the drug-induced kind of ageing is to be embraced with joy. "Pfff," I say to the younger members of my company, "I can't understand this technology/software stuff at all, you will have to do it," They do not believe a word I say but have no choice. I thoroughly enjoy being a difficult older lady around whom others have to tiptoe, as a nice change from a life in the service industry spent being understanding, wise and tolerant of other people. Stuff that.

Climate change? *Après moi le déluge*, as Mme de Pompadour is supposed to have said to Louis XV when signs of the French Revolution grew too large to ignore, but I mean it quite literally. Futuristic scenarios of catastrophe, pestilence, famine, terraforming and endemic idiocy in a lobotomised population of physically isolated but virtually connected techno-serfs makes me feel a bit sorry for my children, but I am sure they will sort it out, and the main thing is that I won't be there to worry about them.

In fact, were Prof E to say to me one day, "Good news, Ileana, we have discovered the cure for your cancer, and you will live for another 30 years," I would be absolutely horrified.

Perhaps my beautiful friend Katherine who just died would not have agreed though. She had been diagnosed with lung cancer over 12 years ago and had been doing everything in her power to stay alive, for the sake of her family almost more than for herself, as the treatments she underwent drained her of all energy and made her feel dreadful a lot of the time. She was definitely not ticking along, she was struggling. We had discussed the pros and cons of keeping going, she said she was very tired of it all, but might as well keep going as her family would be so upset if she gave up.

It sometimes feels like being in the trenches, where your comrades go over the top, and one by one they don't come back. You know one day it will be your turn, but strangely the thought doesn't bother you. Life is good now, and that is all that counts for anyone, and Katherine's struggles are over.

The day after she died, I had an appointment with Prof E. A large and distinguished-looking group was exiting his rooms as I went in. "What a lot of people!" I exclaimed. "Yes," he replied, "The more important the person, the larger the group. Sometimes I have three rows of chairs and a whole line of doctors standing at the back and I feel I am giving a lecture, not seeing a patient. That is when you know it is a really important person."

"Oh dear," I said, "I always see you alone, so I guess I am just a nobody." Prof E gave me a special hug and said, "If it is any consolation, your notes take the longest to read through."

That was of course a huge consolation – every girl likes to feel special, though in the wake of Katherine pulling rank on all of us – when he asked about side effects and if I had anything to report, I just said with complete sincerity, "No, no, all is good, I am fine. I am absolutely fine," and we sat there, just the two of us, smiling happily at each other.

Cancer in the Time of Coronavirus

The world that was on the point of turning upside down in January 2020, when I had triggered a very early Covid-19 scare in hospital, was by March completely topsy turvy, though not in a way that I could have foreseen. I am not especially vulnerable to mass hysteria, thanks to my mother's education, and am by nature an optimistic ostrich-type who believes that sand is an excellent place into which one should stick one's head when

133

things get tricky, so the Armageddon anxiety and doomsday prophecies bounced off me with a quick shake of the feathers. Worldometers is a website which I encourage my friends to explore. You can see the live, digital speedometer of human births and total population total rising every half second, which is even scarier than the thought of losing a couple of million people a few years prematurely. You can also see the number of forest acres lost every half second, which makes one wonder if the odd slowdown in the rate of rising population isn't to be fervently wished for once a year. No, the thought of a very nasty flu epidemic did not faze me. What threw me totally was the shift in how cancer patients were perceived. In normal times, the severer your cancer, the further it has metastasised, the higher the number of drugs you have been through, the higher your status. I enjoy very high status, and I say enjoy intentionally, especially as most of the time I feel pretty well indeed. Obviously, those at death's door have the ultimate high status, but at a certain point, one's social climbing need not be pursued to the very summit. Covid-19 turned this on its head.

"Cancer patients on their fourth line of treatment," I read, (of which I am one, and is usually a token of cancer aristocracy), "Should rather think of spending their last months at home, a quality death, rather than using up valuable resources in the hospital."

From being one of the medical elites, I was suddenly expendable, disposable, to be put in a black dustbin outside the door, on the say-so of some public servant. The realisation that the serene relationship I enjoyed with my mortality was not as rock solid as I thought, was also a shock. What threw my whole philosophy into question was the thought that I was being told by a bureaucrat how, when and where to die, which is the ultimate loss of control. My serenity stemmed from the fact that actually, I felt very well and was going to live for quite a while longer. I was too healthy, too busy, too badly needed to be called expendable. That evening, around midnight, an encrypted email arrived from the clinic. It might as well have been a black-edged death announcement envelope. My heart stood still and I felt dizzy. This was my marching order, my "Dear Ileana, we have enjoyed having you as a patient but sadly you no longer qualify for treatment. People with Covid-19 are higher status than you, so you must now step down. Please stay at home and take paracetamol if you feel unwell or contact us for Counselling."

I slowly opened the layers of encryption and read the letter from Prof E.

"Dear Ileana," it went, "It was nice to see you last week and as discussed, your immune system is doing just fine so there is no need to interrupt your treatment for fear of catching Covid-19. See you in two weeks."

I wrote back to his secretary that very second saying that I had thought they were firing me. "As if!" came the reply one minute later, in three layers of encryption.

Self-isolation doesn't really change things for those living with cancer – we have always been ready to stay home and reduce all appointments; doctors, treatment and hairdresser being the main necessary outings. We go to bed early, take on less, see fewer people, so the only real change is that you have to obey one or more tyrannical children who are convinced that a walk to the local greengrocer will kill you, and stand guard like a pack of Cerebuses on steroids.

"You look very pretty, Mummy, where do you think you are going?"

"Why are you wearing a coat?"

"You didn't seriously just suggest that your cousin Maria come for a walk with the dogs, did you?"

"Why have you put mascara on?"

"Did you wipe those letters with Dettol before bringing them into the house?"

"DON'T TOUCH THAT!!!" and so on.

Not being allowed to go to the supermarket also leaves you particularly vulnerable to any weakness in their ability to follow a shopping list.

"I didn't think you meant one kilo of mince, so I bought some sour cream and chive crisps instead."

"I couldn't find the vegetable aisle."

"There are two apples in the fridge already, so I didn't buy any more fruit."

"Look what I bought instead of garlic!!"

"Sorry, I forgot the eggs, but I did get a couple of pizzas."

"Oh, I didn't see that we already have a crate of Peri-peri sauce... yes, I bought that last time, I remember now." *[And the time before]*

"But it *says* butter on the packet! Oh, I see, it says 'tastes like butter.'"

When this is followed by "What's for supper?" your answer of, "Sour cream and chive crisps with Peri-peri sauce and a quarter of an apple," is delivered with a certain amount of cruelty as you go up for an early night to catch up on *Suits* series seven on Netflix.

The clear solution is to resume the foraging that you practiced in the early days of chemo – so nettle soup, sautéed nettles, nettle pie, wild garlic pesto, nettle pesto, nettle risotto, sorrel sauce, sorrel and wild garlic smoothies, some feathers, earthworms and blades of grass have all returned to the menu. Luckily you did manage to stock-pile some surplus loo paper. Roll on summer and a glut of kale. That will teach them to find the vegetable aisle.

Covid-regulated Harley St waiting rooms offer a much-reduced level of entertainment too, as masked people without accompanying families sit warily in silence. I did take pleasure, though, in a girl who did not realise that her phone was on speaker and spent 15 minutes being unbelievably indiscreet about a friend while repeating that this was all highly confidential, and no one must know. The receptionist vainly tried to signal to her that we could hear, but luckily, she paid no attention and the usual wait for Prof E's appointment passed enjoyably. There was also an unexpected treat in store as Prof E emerged from his room. He looked extraordinarily pleased with himself, and grinning from ear to ear, gave me a twirl.

"How do I look?" he asked coquettishly. He was wearing a mask, goggles, blue surgical gloves and a white plastic pinafore.

"Um, like a lunch lady?" I replied.

"It's the new regulation wear," he explained, and vanished back into his room.

"Ileana," said his secretary a few minutes later, "The lunch lady is now ready to treat your cancer."

After a couple of months, the press started losing interest in Covid deaths and started fretting about other health conditions that for too long had been ignored, so the normal pecking order slowly started to re-establish itself, thank goodness. Getting to the top of the medical pile involves years of hard work, networking and patience, and the established elite feels a certain resentment towards these Johnny-come-latelies, who in a very flashy and nouveau-riche way, queue-barge their way into the clinics, take over our facilities, our drugs, our equipment, our nurses, and then after two weeks disappear again. It is as if our peaceful continent has suddenly been invaded by wide-boys driving corvettes. But they don't last long; one way or another they vanish as quickly as they came. Easy come, easy go. "Tourists!" as we permanent residents say to each other with a curl of the lip.

Normal status restored, I noted with satisfaction that my relationship with mortality had also returned to its customary state of serenity. But I had learned one thing; I can contemplate the skull in the bottom right-hand corner of the painting in tranquillity, but what I am not remotely ready for is someone threatening to whip the rug out from under my feet *in order to give it to someone else not of my choosing and who has not put in the years of work that I have*. I haven't got there yet. If anyone is to decide when I die, it will be me thank you very much. I also realised that I have achieved a certain comfortable familiarity with the idea that what will eventually carry me off will be cancer. My cancer, my personal cancer that has been dancing with me for a long time, who understands me, respects me, *is* me. I feel a calm sense of everything being arranged, of knowing what is going to happen, I expect that a certain sedate and orderly dignity will prevail. What I am not ready for, is to be mugged by an unknown, vulgar, pre-pubescent lout like Covid.

No Pressure...

One morning, after a sleepless night and an unusually strong coffee to get me up and to Harley St for treatment and running the gauntlet of countless Covid-19-era thermometers shoved in one's ear, hand washing stations and mask fittings, I finally

137

settled down in my seat. "Your blood pressure is off the chart." said Tino, "What have you been doing?"

It was the middle of lockdown – what had I been doing?? Reading the news, vacuuming, dishwashing, dusting, ironing, cooking, disinfecting, mopping, laundering, cancelling clients' travel trips, arranging refunds, trying to make sense of our government's experimental and chaotic travel edicts, keeping the family peace, picking kilos of nettles, and trying to run a business. What did they think I had been doing?

"We can't start your treatment till your blood pressure comes down in case you have a heart attack," said Tino.

So, he watched as I did some deep breathing in an attempt to lower my blood pressure. No difference. The doctor came, gave me a small, pink pill, and said to test again in 20 minutes. Twenty minutes later it was still too high, and to make things even more fraught, the chemist came up to say that she was closing the pharmacy in ten minutes, so if she didn't get the green light, we would all have to go home and try another day.

"Get your blood pressure down, *now!*" said the chemist sternly, giving me a rather Maggie Thatcher look, and what seemed like the entire staff, all waiting to go home, stood over me, watching with unblinking anticipation as I tried to think calming thoughts. Two minutes before the deadline, they said that my blood pressure was moving in the right direction at least, and I just shouldn't pick any fights with a taxi driver or family member till the evening.

As instructed, I bought a home blood pressure test kit and started monitoring myself. The readings got higher and higher – to the point where just looking at the damn thing made me break out into a sweat. After a week of my spectacularly hypertensive reports, my cardiologist slotted me in for an emergency cardiograph. My blood pressure was perfect, everything was fine, so when I got home, I threw away the monitor with force into the recycling bin. As the Home Secretary, Priti Patel famously observed – if you shut the shops, the shoplifting problem goes away – and as Donald Trump confirmed, if you don't test people for Covid-19, you get a lower number of reported incidents. They are both quite right and very wise people. My blood pressure was impeccable again as soon as I disposed of the damn machine.

Rather surprisingly, when my cardiologist called to find out the results, he did not share my opinion on this, and arranged for me to be fitted with a professional blood pressure monitor. This is a cuff that you wear for 24 hours, which inflates every half hour and reads your blood pressure, storing the results in a box that hangs around your neck. You must stand stock-still whenever it inflates, rather like the game of Grandmother's footsteps, and it is a nuisance. You are in a queue, about to pay for your groceries, when suddenly the cuff burrs and starts inflating – and you have to freeze, explaining to the customers behind you that you are really sorry, but could they kindly wait 30 seconds while your blood pressure gets taken...

On top of this, a really prissy design (with overtones of control-freakery) means that you can't see the results. Only the cardiology clinic can. The prissy designers did have one trick up their sleeve (or rather, up the patient's sleeve), which is that the tube connecting the cuff to the monitor which hangs around your neck, is blood-red. This means that any length of tube poking out from your shirt looks as if it is full of blood and this has the very satisfactory effect in times of social distancing of clearing the seats next to you on the Underground. It also made my haemophobic daughter go faint and gag when I got home. In all, it is best just to stay home till the 24 hours are up.

The end result was that my blood pressure was absolutely perfect, and Dr L wrote a very professional letter to the Oncology clinic saying that I had "White Coat Hypertension", which sounds serious but just means that I take one look at Tino and the gang in the clinic, and my BP goes up...

Little League

I was contacted via Facebook by Colette, a beautiful girl from Lancashire who was, in her words, "just riddled with it," and who told me about all the MBC Facebook groups that one could join. I had to ask what MBC meant, which showed me just how out of date and low-status I was becoming. Colette sweetly explained that it meant Metastatic Breast Cancer, and sent me a photo of her poodle, Babette, trying to join her in her personal HBOT – yes, I had to google that too – it is a Hyperbaric Oxygen Treatment capsule – a cutting edge treatment for very advanced cancer and very high-status residents of Cancerland – the highest aristocracy. Newly humbled, I joined the first MBC Facebook group I found; a large group of vocal ladies, run primarily from Florida. I realised that I was well out of my league. Amazing women, off of whose tongues tripped all the longest drug names and who seemed to have the most complicated phenotypes of cancer:

"I was Her 2 triple negative."

"I was Her 2 triple negative AND Her 2 triple positive."

"I was ER/PR +Her2, plus Pik3, ERBB", Pten, AN receptors."

"I have had ten treatments, three chemos, two targets, and six trials."

"My oncologist says I am a unicorn!"

I realise that it is my bad character and not anything intended by the kind ladies sharing their histories, but it did trigger my competitive streak; in an effort to join in and not be outgunned by a bunch of Yanks, I played my only trump card:

"Is anyone here on T-DM1s, like me?" I asked casually, knowing that very few would have even heard of it as it was so new.

"?"

"It is a teeny weeny, highly toxic chemo bomblet," I went on proudly, "that hitches a ride on a Herceptin molecule to find a cancer cell, then it slides inside and blows it up!"

"Wow, that is a cool visualisation," came the kind reply, "but don't you mean Trastuzumab- Emtansine? The T-DM1 molecule isn't usually given with Herceptin."

I looked at my treatment record booklet, and had to agree that yes, that is in fact exactly what I did mean. I had got it wrong – I didn't even know what my own treatment was called, for heaven's sake. In fact, I had been filling out my insurance forms for a year with the wrong drug. Not that they noticed or minded.

"Chemo brain," whooshed in the very generous response from the group when I admitted my failure to know anything at all.

As a final insult, it became clear from the Facebook group, that not only was I living in a small, provincial cul-de-sac of Cancerland UK, but those in the prime residential areas of Cancerland USA actually had "pain management nurses" who advised them on how to deal with pain and supplied them with exotic drugs including cannabis. All I ever got was paracetamol.

The next day I had a call from my cardiologist mentioning that my high blood pressure might be a result of the Herceptin I am taking.

"Dr L," I said somewhat sternly, "I must correct you, I am not on Herceptin anymore, I am on Trastuzumab-Emtansine."

"Trastumuzab is the brand name for Herceptin," he said kindly.

So, there we have it. I was right after all, and not in a chemo-brain muddle. Or rather, I was in an even worse chemo-brain muddle than I thought, but I don't think I will update that scary Facebook group. I spent the next few weeks liking and hearting every post in a gesture of submission while I re-grouped myself.

***

On the subject of Yanks, I was idly chatting to an American friend of mine who lives in London and by coincidence, is also a patient of Prof E. She was trying to identify what made it unlikely that an American would write a funny book about cancer. My view was that, unlike the highly secular British, America is a fundamentally religious nation with a natural affinity to revere things approved by a higher authority, be that Twitter, God, Oprah Winfrey, or other. This reverence is extended to all sort of things; from Hollywood stars and their utterances to taboos, and cancer is definitely a taboo. I do sincerely respect my cancer – I made it after all, and it is very much a part of me – but that doesn't mean I have to bow at its altar.

The American fear of taboos has an interesting side-effect, which is that they also prefer to be part of a group in order to express opinions. Security in numbers. You don't want to meet a taboo all on your own on a dark night.

The US education system, to British eyes at least, seems to further encourage this "belonging" notion. You score points in US colleges just for class participation. Do you have nothing individual or new to say? It doesn't matter, just raise your hand and endorse someone's point of view, and you gain lots of points, and are considered to have made a valuable contribution to a discussion, which is a source of amazement to the Brits who traditionally have seen no particular merit in agreeing with anyone. British Exceptionalism, I think it is called.

I remember a summit sponsored by a major American travel magazine that I attended a couple of times in New York. We five British participants sat in the back row and didn't dare open our mouths, as we realised that anything we said that was a little flippant or in disagreement with the group would be met with disapproving silence or a sharp intake of the collective breath. We learned to put up our hands and say, "I would just like to say that Joel made a great point there." And then bask in the approval when someone else would put up their hand and say, "I would just like to say that I agree with Ileana that Joel made a great point there", until the chain got so long that it broke under its own weight and was finally replaced by someone else making a new great point, which was inevitably that he bought subscriptions to that magazine for all his friends every Christmas. This would then unleash a whole soccer-wave of hand-putting-up and, "My name is Jules, and I just want to say what a great idea that is of Jack's, and I will do the same", and "My name is Jill, and I just want to add that I agree with Jules that that is a great idea of Jack's, and I too will be copying it". "Hi, I am Jim, and I would like to say that Jack had a great idea, and I agree with Jules and Jill, and I too will be gifting a subscription to my clients at Christmas," and this would go on for what seemed an age. Everyone was happy, and in the back row, we five Brits stuffed our fists in our mouths to stop getting the giggles, like rebellious ten-year-olds.

By contrast, there was the unforgettable moment where, at a French travel summit, the French keynote speaker held up his hand for the silence he required to make an important point, and announced to the 800-strong audience in portentous tones,

"We all know zat money cannot buy a penis."

This again reduced us Brits in the back row to paroxysms of laughter while Jim and Jack held their breath, understandably unsure about whether to put up their hands and agree with this or not... sheer torture for them. What the speaker meant, of course, was the trite and yet inaccurate "Money can't buy happiness," or, as it came out in his French accent, "Money cannot buy 'appiness". His point was spectacularly untrue whichever way you interpreted it, especially in Marrakech, where the travel summit was being held. It is best to leave American groupthink to the Americans.

I adore the USA and lived for two very happy and somewhat squalid years as a theatre design student in New York, the details of which my parents luckily knew very little. I love my American friends, I work with American agents, journalists and clients and have been doing so for 20 years, but Americans are not like the British, as one is sometimes fooled into thinking by our similar language. If they spoke Cherokee, we would realise what an exotic country it really is in every way. I worked one long summer as a student scenic artist in an amateur theatre-camp in the Black Hills of South Dakota and marvelled at the individuality and creativity – often drug enhanced, of my fellow students there. They filled me with admiration. We had a camp drug supplier who drove up from Custer every second Monday with our orders, there was a witch who found four leaf clovers for everyone on opening nights, there was the camp director's 1950's Doris-Day-style southern belle wife, who was also the camp slut, and there was an inventive team in the camp kitchens who memorably dyed the bacon, grits, scrambled eggs and baked beans blue one morning. There were the hash brownies for tea one day, which I hadn't understood were hash brownies, of which I gobbled down half a dozen as I have always been greedy. This would have been fine, but the set-designer then came to find the paint team – me and a blond Iowan who was even more out of it than I was – and asked us to quickly mix a tiny quantity of mushroom-coloured paint with which to redo some fine *trompe l'oeil* panels in a wall. I had a crush on the blond Iowan, so heroically volunteered to do it myself. The designer watched in bafflement as I sat there slowly pouring randomly chosen buckets of paint into each other, spending ten minutes looking at my paint brush to see which end was which, while the blond Iowan carefully glued the ruler at an artistic slant to the backdrop. The designer did it himself in the end, and I had to explain the next day.

"I love hash brownies," he said crossly, "Why wasn't I given any?"

Then there was the day the entire crew, except for me, got drunk and trashed a spot in the forest that is sacred to the Sioux, and then the next day all came down with a mysterious stomach bug – again, except for me.

The vast spaces in the middle of the USA are the cradle of American dynamism and enterprise, but, and this is the key point, unless those kids managed to escape marrying their childhood sweetheart and migrated to one of the coasts, the game was up before they were 30. I see the vast interior of America as the centre of a massive centrifugal force that scatters its talent out towards the coasts. The brain between the two ears.

***

Whether or not my analysis of US versus UK mindsets is correct, it was crystal clear that irreverence in the MBC Facebook groups would go down like a lead balloon. I did experiment though; one lady posted to ask if anyone else was experiencing "cognitive deterioration" and what could one do about it. I replied that chemo brain is a well-known side effect, but one can fight it, explaining my strategy of reading books on quantum physics.

"It really works," I wrote, "I can't remember what that white thing in the kitchen is called, the one where I keep food that needs to stay cold, but I can explain multiverses to whoever is interested." No one was interested in hearing about the multiverse, nor did anyone helpfully supply the name of the large, white, electric object in my kitchen, and I felt that old travel-summit disapproving silence and heard again that sharp intake of the collective breath.

144

Undeterred, my next attempt was to jump into an exchange between a lady who wanted to know how to disguise some bald patches as she gave herself a fright every time, she caught sight of herself in the mirror, and someone who was telling her that she was beautiful in herself and didn't need to do anything. I wrote that of course we are all beautiful in ourselves, but a little L'Oréal hair powder can only help. I mean why not? It makes us beautiful on the outside as well as the inside and is so much easier than having to repeat both to ourselves and to others that one is beautiful inside. That didn't go down very well at all. To play safe, my next post from the back row of the MBC group was to hold up my hand and volunteer a helpful tip on home-made icepacks for itchy scalps. Harmony was mostly restored – but I will persevere. I see it as my mission. Row of caring-hug emojis. Speaking of which, we could do with some cancer-friendly emojis... just for starters, how about: hot flashes, can't remember, itchy, creaky, sore, sleepless at 4 am, sofa day, I need a neck rub and entertain me. Would Apple please oblige – and while they are at it, make them bigger – I recently did a patriotic Facebook post to boost Greek tourism, but managed to embellish it with a row of Argentinian flags instead of Greek ones. Very embarrassing, and now the office is calling me Evita.

Major League

After a few weeks of following the posts from these Facebook groups, and getting to know the faces and circumstances of my virtual cancer friends, I began to feel a little guilty and ashamed by my frivolity in the face of so much pain, unhappiness, misery, bravery and fear. The urge to joke suddenly weakened. In fact, I felt completely humbled, as if I were a child playing in kindergarten, while the adults were having a serious conversation in the room above. Perhaps it was time to put aside childish things and take a more serious view. Perhaps I should focus on trying to become a more empathetic person and force myself to contemplate the abyss. Perhaps the others are right –one should not distract oneself, or upset people dealing with serious matters by relentlessly finding things to laugh at. Perhaps the joke was not very funny after all. Perhaps it was even time to stop writing. At the very least to quit Facebook.

The next morning, the cracks that I had felt in my tectonic plates, just as I had felt in the Dolomites with my daughter, had settled down again, the breath of hot magma and sulphur from below had faded and things returned to normal. I decided that there was nothing to gain from becoming more empathetic and adult, that laughing was simply more fun than being serious, and that the abyss could wait. So I didn't quit Facebook, instead, I asked my Facebook residents of Cancerland USA for their funny stories. You never know. America is the home of some of the most brilliantly irreverent taboo-busters that have ever existed – South Park springs to mind – who can forget the weather alert about the cloud of smug smothering Hollywood around Oscar time?

The first lady to reply to my Facebook request wrote that she had no funny stories. I told her to practice looking for things to laugh at and it would get easier. "I have no problem laughing," she replied crossly, "I just don't have any stories."

Karen, a retired teacher from Ohio, diagnosed 12 years ago, was the next to reply:

"It was a slow day in the chemo office, and there was only one other woman close to me. I was reading a book when I glanced up and saw her light a cigarette. Yes, not a vapey thingy, which would be bad enough, but an actual cigarette! I did a double take, then looked towards the nurses's station. They were all busy and hadn't noticed. Finally, one of them looked up and I caught her eye, gave her a look, and kinda nodded my head towards Cigarette Lady. The nurse's mouth dropped open and she sprinted over, exclaiming, 'What are you doing? You can't smoke!' To which the lady replied, 'Yes I can, the doctor told me I can smoke if I want.' The nurse had to explain that the doctor meant that she could smoke at home but certainly not in the chemo ward."

My mouth dropped open as well at that one, clearly some Cancerland USA residents have some strange ideas…

146

"I forgot to say," added Karen, "That she also managed to pull out her chemo-IV drip when she went to use the bathroom."

I couldn't help wondering if her oncologist, by allowing her to smoke, was trying to hasten Cigarette Lady's final departure from his clinic...

The next story I was sent was not at all funny – well, theoretically it is possible to spin almost anything into a funny story, I dare say I could have done it – but you'd have to dig very deep for this one...

Mary-Anne was shopping in the US. She coughed (a cancer cough), into her arm, explained to the lady behind her – who had jumped back in alarm – that it was cancer, not COVID, and then, to continue in her own words: "I kid you not, the woman said I should stay home and called me a fat bitch. I was shaking with the hurt it caused me." I was struck dumb with how horrible this was.

The replies that came streaming in from other USA Cancerland members were almost as alarming to polite British ears as the original transgression, though of course more justified.

I began to understand why so many people find joking almost in bad taste. When there is so much that needs fixing, so much about which one simply *has* to be judgemental, irreverence seems almost a luxury or a privilege. I am optimistic, though, that with time, practice and careful observation, I will eventually find the right groove and be able to pass for one of the MBC Facebook gang. Adding "girl" to posts, as in "you got this, girl!" is a useful tip, and emojis are pretty safe as well.

I did manage one successful posting:

"Ladies," I wrote, "Do T-DM1s make you grumpy or is it husbands?" Mine had been rather irritating that week and I did rather want to know the answer.

"Husbands," came the replies, thick and fast. One lady wrote sadly that she had lost her husband ten years ago and that today was his birthday (row of hearts and caring hug emojis). One wrote that she wasn't married and wasn't grumpy at all (smug smile emoji), and one husband actually had the temerity to write in on his wife's account to say his wife was a pain in the neck, but he guessed he just had to put up with it. We suggested that he start his own Facebook support group and never show his face in ours again.

Until I get the hang of it though, I will keep a low profile. I did update my status on Facebook though, the details of which I had never really bothered to fill out, and as I had recently celebrated my 32nd wedding anniversary, I wrote "Married" in the status field. Within two minutes the congratulations started streaming in. I spent the next day assuring my friends that I hadn't been dumped by Florian or met anyone else. What absolutely flummoxed me though, was the fact that not one person asked me what had happened to Florian or whom I had married... The pitfalls of social media are never-ending. As however, are the rewards. I treasure the new insights and friends I have made from across the ocean and learn from their cultural perspective. In fact, one of them sweetly volunteered to edit my ruminations concerning the USA to avoid causing offence, an offer I gratefully took her up on. She did so tactfully and intelligently, and I can safely say that any offence still caused is entirely the fault of Sue from North Carolina.

I did get safely home from my travels in the virtual Badlands of the USA, and what is more, relatively unscathed by the soul-searching those travels caused. My encounters with the US sisters have taught me that you don't always need to spray-paint everything with a glittering coat of sparkling laughter. Sometimes, boring as it is, one can just be nice.

Here is what one nice lady wrote to console another lady who had made the mistake of googling her prognosis and felt like giving up:

"99.99 % of you is fine and healthy. You can eat lovely meals, drink good wine, cuddle and walk your pet, love your husband and other family members, enjoy time spent with friends, make new friends, see good movies, hear beautiful music, appreciate a good TV drama, enjoy holidays, new places, new books to read, new shoes to buy and wear!
Did you have a written guarantee that you would live for 90 years? No! Of course not! None of us have any guarantee except that we will die one day. We go through life knowing this, but we don't give up living because we are going to die one day!"

"Stage 4 is a huge wake up call to live every moment in the moment. I have never felt so loved or loved so much these past 14 months. My life has been transformed with the love that's now in it, and that I have allowed in. My four sweet cats and adorable baby poodle make me laugh and give me so much joy. My husband shows his love in his constant care and appreciation, we've fallen in love with each other all over again. Sorry to sound cheesy but I hope, once the terror subsides that you will feel the hope and joy."

At the risk of sounding cheesy myself, these comments remind one that while the power of laughter is amazing, so is the power of love. Love does get tested though. One naïve young entrant to the Facebook group innocently asked if it was safe to have intercourse after chemo. She wasn't showing off apparently, but genuinely asking. There was the sharp intake of breath again as we longer-term Cancerland residents tried to remember what intercourse was, then one of the group wrote back kindly on behalf of all of us,

"Yes, of course it is safe, we just tell our husbands it isn't."

I will maintain right until the end that when you live with a disease that continuously chips away at your physical liberties, the freedom to laugh is the one freedom that stays within your control, that depends on no one, and should be enjoyed no matter how much your children, Facebook or anyone else disapproves. There *are* no taboos, the choice is *always* whether to laugh or to cry, and laughter wins for me each time.

Holiday Time

Following a routine scan to see how my liver was bearing up under the chemo I am on, which is notoriously bad for it, it appeared that my liver was not bearing up quite as well as one might hope. A further MRI was ordered, the one where you pass slowly through a tube while things bang and clang and, if anything metal is in you, it gets pulled out of you by the ultra-strong magnets.

"Breathe IN," said the machine, so I took a deep breath as I like to be good at things.

"Breathe OUT," it then said, so I expelled every last molecule of air from my lungs.

"Now hold your breath."

What? How can you hold your breath when you have none left to hold, and for how long can you go without any air in your body? Twenty-five seconds the machine seemed to think, which I can tell you is absolute nonsense. Fifteen, tops.

In the end, I cheated. I took deep breaths in, then, making a dramatic noise, pretended to breathe out, but really only let a little wisp escape. That way I always had enough breath to hold, and the machine fell for it every time. AI has a long way to go.

At my follow up appointment, Prof E looked at the scan, listened to me rabbiting on about my aches and pains and detailing the ever-growing list of medicines I was taking, then suddenly said,

"You need a holiday."

"Yes," I agreed immediately; that was an easy one.

"I mean your liver needs a holiday."

I am in the holiday business but figuring out how to give my liver a holiday away from the rest of me was a challenge.

Prof E looked at me in a way that said not to try a lame joke on him, so I didn't.

"You have had chemo for four years now, the cancer is in remission, which is really good, brilliant, but your liver is showing signs of damage from the chemo. I have a very strong feeling that we should give you a chemo holiday and stop treatment for around nine weeks."

This is a very mixed message. On the one hand, it is very good that your cancer is so stable that you can afford to stop treatment for a while, but not so good that your liver is threatening to call a halt to proceedings.

Prof E rarely puts his foot down with me, so there was nothing to say. My liver was going to get its holiday.

"I know you are going to Germany now, so have these blood tests done there in two weeks and email me the results," he said, and scribbled a few weird hieroglyphs on the back of an old appointment card with lots of crossings out on it.

"I can't show that to a German doctor!" I protested, "They think Brits are crazy at the best of times."

Prof E squinted at his handiwork and then carefully added a couple of hooks and squiggles to two of the hieroglyphs.

"That's better," he said with satisfaction, "That should be clear to anyone."

The clinic doctor and I managed to keep straight faces till he had left, then the clinic doctor typed out an official letter with headed paper loaded with doctorates and initials and the list of blood tests needed.

"Thank you," I said gratefully, and national honour was saved.

"Cancer cells," I told my body sternly on the way home (I am a superstitious, even pagan Greek deep down, and I talk to my cancer cells so that they feel loved and love me in return. I talk to most things in fact, especially inanimate objects that can't get away or argue with me), "Listen to me carefully. You are to just *sit still* while I am on holiday, do not move, do not see anyone, do not do anything, above all *do not touch anything*, and I will be back soon."

"Gap Year!" chorused my children, when I told them about my holiday, and one of them kindly volunteered to go away with me for a bit, but what to do with my sudden freedom in mid-August in the middle of a pandemic with travel bans and quarantines left, right and centre?

I started dreaming about a little shack on a beach with no one around and Netflix at night, while my sensible self told me that I ought really to go to an austere, Teutonic clinic somewhere and fast, detox, do yoga, have enemas and meditate. Some Gap Year, I thought glumly. In the end, I did go to Germany as planned, stocking up on poppy-seed filled strudels, dumplings and sausages, sent a teutonically efficient blood test back to Prof E, and then headed, as I always do when I need to re-boot, up to the mountains, to the Dolomites, to the crags and rocks, the marmots and minerals, the azure and gold, the glitter, clouds, pine trees, thunder, rain and shadows. I filled my pockets each day with pebbles, rocks and bits of wood, objects that called out to me that they were charged with energy and protective vibrations tailored just for me. Talismans, silence, exercise and apple strudel turn out to be just what my liver wanted, as four weeks later, Prof E said that as the cancer looked stable, we could try the chemo every four weeks instead of three.

"You aren't giving up on me?" I said anxiously, "Will I still be protected?"

"Of course I am not giving up on you, don't be ridiculous. You are doing really well, and we will scan you more closely to make up for less chemo, but with you, I threw the instruction booklet away a long time ago."

I was not sure that it was as reassuring as he meant it to be, but there we are.

"Ah, Prof E," said the clinic manager that afternoon as I was having treatment and explaining my new regime to her. "Chemotherapy is an art, not a science, and Prof E is its Picasso."

Hopefully I won't end up blue, with two wonky eyes on the same side of my face spurting tears all over the shop, and my nose sticking out at a weird angle.

Close Encounters

Lockdown doesn't overly affect us Cancerland residents – from the social point of view anyway – in fact, there appeared a whole array of things to do at home that had not been on offer before. My favourite of these is an online yoga website that I have subscribed to, which tailors yoga routines especially for you. I choose the six-minute ones as I have a low boredom threshold, then I lie on my bed, propped up with lots of pillows and a cup of tea, and watch energetic and highly motivated American girls with swingy ponytails and ripped torsos, gleaming with sweat and panting, while they exhort me with excited yips of "Good jaaahb, you gaaaht this!" and "Wow, you rully, rully crushed that," as I reach for another chocolate biscuit. Absolutely spot on. I really have got this. I am crushing it. Very relaxing and uplifting, as they promise. My body is energised, my mind de-stresses, and I sleep much better after watching a couple of workouts. Soon I will try the 20-minute work outs – one has to build up to these things gradually, no point overdoing it to start with.

Living at close quarters with the family (who have all moved back in), has revealed some interesting traits. My sister Paola has been having lockdown dreams. In one of them she is attending a concert given by the Angel Gabriel. He looks, she says, just like Barry Manilow in a long, black leather coat. He invites her into his private jet (his wings?), and then says that she should ask him the three most meaningful questions about life – the questions that will explain all the mysteries of the universe to her. She asks them. He answers. Then she wakes up and can remember neither the questions nor the answers, but, in her waking struggle to remember, she hears a voice (not Barry Manilow this time, I asked just to be clear, more like Bob Dylan), saying "You are not ready to hear the answers." "Bugger" she says to herself.

My daughter Danae has also been active on the spiritual side: her crystals now encrust every surface, gleaming and flashing from every table-top and shelf, even encroaching into the kitchen. I didn't think my cooking needed extra help, but perhaps she is sending me a message with her malachite shards glowering at me from the spice rack. Tendrils of sprouting plants occupy any space not taken up by crystals, other than the corner of the boiler room, which is where she makes slightly sulphurous-tasting, fizzy Kefir from a kit she ordered online. A jar of pallid grub-like lumps are the starter bacteria, that one feeds with fruit juice or milk or whatever. "Aren't they sweet!" she coos lovingly at them, and the jars proliferate, fizzing ominously if touched.

**

Across the way, my very elderly neighbour, one of the last remaining survivors of the notorious *kindertransport*, was evacuated from Vienna in 1938 as an eight-year-old refugee, and began life in England sitting on her suitcase in King's Cross Station like Paddington Bear, waiting for a host family who never turned up. She is a charming and coquettish widow who sadly lost her only daughter to cancer a few years ago. A clear survivor, she has been telling me wistfully every day for the last five years that she wants to die.

153

"Why can't I die? I am lonely, I have nothing to live for, and I just want to fade away quietly in my bed at home."

Well, she did manage to contract Covid, in spite of never going out. This caused her great fatigue but nothing else, and it looked, as she lay in bed like a tiny, frail sparrow, that she would indeed get her wish and just slip away peacefully at home. Every day masked and gloved, I would go over with chicken broth (duly rejected as too weak/too strong/too salty/too bland) and sit a while with her and look as empathetic as I could. But it soon turned out that fading away peacefully at home was not what she wanted at all. She wanted a private doctor to visit every day. She wanted consultants to visit every other day. She wanted to be admitted to hospital, she wanted to be admitted to a hospice, she wanted every resource known to science to be thrown at her. In case we thought she was too demanding, there were also lots of things that she didn't want. She didn't want the night nurse to live in, as she was sure that she snooped in her desk. She didn't want the day nurse to talk to her in that annoying voice. She didn't want the replacement nurse to answer the phone. She didn't want to brush her teeth, and she didn't want to use the hospital bed provided. She didn't want to give anyone a power of attorney. And once she had recovered, she wanted to know why it had all cost so much and why I was allowing our other elderly neighbour to interfere with fixing the potholes in the drive.

"Ghastly man," she emailed me, "If he doesn't like the road, he should move out. And his wife runs an illegal clinic from the house, I am sure." She then copied him in by mistake... She will outlive me, I am sure.

Supporting this conviction is the little known but interesting fact that bad-tempered or waspish people do apparently outlive sweet and placid people (not that I am particularly sweet and placid, I should say, before anyone else does). The rush of adrenaline they get from complaining or saying something mean, it seems, is very healthy. My widowed grandmother, who was the very model of placid positivity and stoicism, died aged 83. Her widowed sister, with whom she lived in an uneasy state of peace (separate kitchens was the key), was known for her wicked tongue and delight in troublemaking. She lived till 103, writing waspishly to her 94-year-old brother who said that he couldn't make her 100th birthday party, "Never mind Walter, I will come to yours."

My other sister, Marina, and I have been discussing funeral arrangements – or rather, what music we want played.

"I want everyone to be in floods of tears all the time, so I have chosen all the saddest songs I can think of so that even you will cry." said Marina.

"But I don't want to cry," I objected. "If you are going to have a lot of tear-jerking German Lieder, I won't come."

"Oh, come on, Dido's Lament, by Monteverdi," she persisted, "The lament she sings as she commits suicide after being abandoned by Aeneas. You have to cry at that."

"I certainly won't," I said, "I mean, seriously, imagine your last words being *'Remember me, remember me,'* So needy, so, so needy…"

"You are heartless," she said crossly. "Well, then, at the end I am going to have Elvis singing 'Peace in the Valley' – that will make you cry."

"Peace in the Valley, with you there?" I said, "that is a fond hope… it will be crash, bang, whistle and stomp in the Valley once you get there. Rather have them play 'Who Let the Dogs Out?' and then I will feel guilty at having shouted at you so often for having done that."

"Oh, alright," Marina agreed, "Guilt trip it is then. Whatever it takes. What are you going to have?"

"'Three Little Birds' by Bob Marley, 'Lovely Day' by Bill Withers, and for the final procession out, 'Give Me Sunshine' sung by Morcombe and Wise."

"That's ridiculous," she protested, "Don't you want people to be sad?"

"I trust they will be sad anyway, and as I have a very kind heart and am a Libran people-pleaser, I want to cheer them up."

"Hmphh," said Marina, "Ridiculous."

A Not Very Funny Thing Happened
on the Way to Chemo

As a footnote, the "ghastly neighbour", who has been nagging me for months about fixing the potholes on our drive, and whose threats of litigation I ignore as I consider his speeding a much greater danger to man and beast than any mere hole in the ground, has finally won the argument. Walking gaily down to the station on my way to having my six-monthly PET scans, I fell into the deepest pothole there was. Before my eyes a grapefruit-sized ball swelled up over my ankle, and I hopped back home to get crutches and find someone to drive me to Harley St. Having been dropped off as close to Harley St as the car could go, I started swinging my way down to number 81. Crutches with chemo-fibromyalgia in the shoulders are no fun at all, my ankle was still swelling, and at number 143 I gave up, crying with pain. A taxi stood at the curb invitingly, with a kindly-looking cabbie at the wheel. I looked at him in what I hoped was a winning, teary-eyed, Princess Diana-like way over my mask, explained the agony I was in, and asked if he could be my angel, my saviour, and just take me 50 yards down the road. "Of course," he said, "hop in", and drove me all of five seconds down the road. He opened the door for me tenderly and, as I hopped out, I thanked him most sincerely. "God bless you," I said, "That was a kindness to a poor crippled lady, and thank you again from the bottom of my heart. Really, God bless, and have a lovely day."

"Oi," he said sharply. "That will be £4.50." What stung me most, as I handed over the money while saying "You are having a laugh, mate", was the fact that I had asked God to bless him. Twice.

"Cancel!" I telegraphed skywards, but I am not sure how good the back office is up there. Amazon doesn't run it after all.[†]

[†] In a celestial moment of karma, the taxi driver the next day refused to take any money off me. I insisted, saying that heaven had sent him to make up for his colleague of the day before. This time I was the one who got the "God bless." All very satisfactory.

Getting from one clinic to the other was also not unproblematic. "Yes," said the receptionist of Number 81, "We have a wheelchair to take you to Number 157, but the porters won't wheel you without a Healthcare Professional escorting and it will take us some time to find a porter and a Healthcare Professional both free at the same time. Covid, you know, we are understaffed."

I felt another "You are having a laugh mate" moment coming over me. Then I saw Dimitris, a Greek nurse, lurking nearby. "Dimitris," I whispered to him in Greek, "Let's do this the Greek way and make a break for it. You grab one of those wheelchairs and let's go, it is only one block away."

"We're off!" I called to the receptionist as Dimitris seized the wheel of our getaway chair.

"Oh my, Dimitris, are you sure you will be OK?" she called after us in a panic.

Dimitris and I looked at each other.

"She has never worked in Greece," said Dimitris and we both creased with laughter. An elderly couple, holding hands and walking at a snail's pace ahead of us blocked the pavement, oblivious to our hisses of impatience behind them, or perhaps just with the hearing aids turned down. Greek wheelchairs probably come with horns, but not British ones, so the rest of my journey was conducted in a sedate and very un-Greek fashion.

The Radiology clinic, to which I have been going twice a year for five years, retained its perfect record of cocking something up each time I visit, as those of you who have been following my stories will know. This time it was a double whammy – no record of my appointment, ("You will have to go home and come back tomorrow"), and a missing insurance claim cover. I assured them that whoever was going to be sent home and told to come back the next day, that person was not going to be me. I had probably broken my foot trying to get there, had just paid for a five second taxi ride, stolen a wheelchair, might be bed-bound for days – and so, while under normal circumstances I would have beamed forgivingly at them, meekly agreeing to their demands – as it happened, this time I was going to sit right there and complain loudly till they scanned me.

They are almost used to me by now, so they suddenly discovered a cancellation, and all was fine.

As a bonus, one of those wonderful Harley St scenes was unfolding in front of me as I waited for my turn. A heavily veiled lady with a pair of scared eyes peeping out through her niqab, who spoke no English, was being prepped for her CT scan injection. She was being aided to a questionable degree by the interpreting abilities of her husband, whose English was marginally better. I guess the official interpreters were also Covid-struck. The nurse was making valiant efforts to mime to the lady that the injections would create a warm feeling spreading between her thighs and down her legs, and she might think that she had urinated on herself. It was worth every minute of the 40-minute hold-up this caused. Whoever said that charades was a boring game? Just watching, I stifled so much laughter that I myself nearly created a warm feeling spreading between my thighs and down my legs.

When my turn did come, the very nice radiologist kindly scanned my foot as well as the prescribed parts, whilst he was at it.

"Not broken," he smiled happily.

"Isn't it refreshing to have a scanee who couldn't care less about the cancer results and just wants to know about a sprained ankle?" I asked. He said it was indeed, bustled me out of the clinic, and I bet that they all heaved a huge sigh of relief. As it happens, he was wrong as I found out a few days later that it was broken, so now I feel that my bad behaviour was entirely justified.

Ticking Along

If I have made Cancerland sound as if it is sometimes fun, that is because it can be, and more often than one might think. Any country can be fun for some of the time. Well, perhaps not any country... Tom, he of the mother-in-law and knackered knees, had just had two new titanium knees put in and was looking to join the cool gang.

"Would you like me to write a paragraph for you about Kneeland?" he suggested one day with unforgiveable pushiness.

"Absolutely not," I replied indignantly, "Kneeland sounds like a downmarket sports outlet in Ohio and I am writing a serious book here about a serious illness. What next? Ingrown-toenailland or Haemorrhoidland?"

There is not a bandwagon around onto which some people won't try to jump, even if they have just had titanium knees put in and shouldn't be jumping on anything. Cancerland is an elite and superior country with borders and territorial integrity to defend, and all its inhabitants are scarred and battle-hardened, so don't fool with us. Kneeland my foot.

***

After five years, life in Cancerland has settled down into a humdrum routine, and I am, as Prof E says with satisfaction, "ticking along". This always has a slightly alarming echo of a ticking bomb where someone has lit the fuse and legged it for shelter, to watch the explosion from a safe place, which is also not a bad metaphor for us who live with cancer – life ticking away until the bomb goes off. Tick, tick, tick, tick, tick, tick, tick, BOOOM. I have travelled around the continent, learned to love my new home, to value its customs and inhabitants, to examine its flora and fauna, wander its paths and wildernesses. I am, for now, comfortably settled again in the leafy suburb of Remission, though I keep my suitcases somewhere where I can easily reach them. My collection of tales, the postcards I write, will, I hope, continue to keep me happy, and the inevitable bumps in the road will continue to be navigated with calm, by Prof E at least. I often read that being told to be positive is distressing for people who are ill or depressed, and I fully understand that – it is cruel to put pressure on someone to emanate like a ray of sunshine when they are not really feeling like it. You can't do that on command, I certainly couldn't. For me, a sunny disposition is the side effect of my personal conviction that I am a lucky person. This is quite different from being positive. It is being able to see clearly how much worse things could be, which is the truth for most of us. It is that feeling of luckiness which makes me believe that a treatment will work, that a scan will be clear, that side effects can be tolerated, it is not a decision on my part to be positive. I don't mean the kind of luckiness that wins us lottery tickets, which I have never won in my life. I mean the kind of luckiness that has already given most of us so much more than might have been the case.

Hurting my foot on the way to being scanned was, for me, an enormous stroke of luck. I mean, just imagine. I was on my way to the doctor anyway and even got an unscheduled, instant diagnosis (even if it turned out to be wrong), and wheelchair transport. How lucky is that? Imagine if I had been on my way to the dentist or supermarket or post office. Friends texting me in sympathy saying how awful for me, missed the point entirely.

In the back of my mind is a pre-war Austrian-Jewish aunt in Vienna, Tante Jolesch, about whom her nephew wrote a lovely book. It is a source of profoundly wise thoughts, such as "to whatever extent a man is better looking than an ape, is a luxury". Pithier in German of course. One day, fed up with the habitual chorus of "what a stroke of luck" from her superstitious family when anyone described a narrowly averted accident, death or bankruptcy – on hearing someone recount the latest mishap, followed inevitably by 'what a stroke of luck!' – she snapped,

"God save us all from any more strokes of luck!"

In spite of that, if I were asked to distil my wisdom into something short and concise (easy enough as there is really not much of it to distil), I would still say that my lodestar, my golden key, is to remember that there is so much to be grateful for and, as even Tante Jolesch would admit, we are all lucky in so many ways. Discovering those many ways is the reward that awaits those who search, in Cancerland or elsewhere. We Cancerlanders will continue for as long as we are given, to eat (nothing with sugar though), drink (bitter green juices), and make merry (though only until around 10.30pm which is definitely bedtime in Cancerland), and say thank you at the beginning and end of every day, to all those who look after us and love us, for all our blessings, and for everything that keeps us smiling.

Acknowledgements

As before, my thanks go to the amazing people who look after my health and allow themselves to appear in these pages – Paul Ellis and the ladies who make sure he functions properly, Alexander Lyon, Richard Marley, Neal Navani, Michael Harding, and of course the team at Number 81 headed by the magnificent Louise. My pit-stop is full of the kind of skilled mechanics who ought to be looking after Ferraris rather than an old family sedan.

Thanks to Robert Moeginger for continuing with patience and good humour to navigate his way through the – to Germans – incomprehensible mess that is UK health billing practices.

Huge thanks to Helena Sutcliffe for her dextrous editing which made this a better book than it would have been otherwise (in fact, without Helena there would have been no book at all), and to my friends and family for putting up with me and loving me in spite of everything. I love them all too.

Printed in Great Britain
by Amazon

10240920R00098